EVERYDAY HEROES

HEROES

OF THE

QUALITY

MOVEMENT

EVERYDAY HEROES

HEROES

OF THE

QUALITY

MOVEMENT

From Taylor to Deming–
The Journey to Higher Productivity

Perry Gluckman
Diana Reynolds Roome

FOREWORD BY
Dr. W. Edwards Deming

DORSET HOUSE PUBLISHING
353 West 12th Street, New York, NY 10014

Library of Congress Cataloging-in-Publication Data

Gluckman, Perry, 1938-1992.
    Everyday heroes of the quality movement : from Taylor to
Deming, the journey to higher productivity / by Perry Gluckman & Diana
Reynolds Roome ; foreword by W. Edwards Deming, with an introduction
to the second edition by Ken Delavigne. -- 2nd ed.
    p.   cm.
    Rev. ed. of: Everyday heroes. 1989.
    ISBN 0-932633-26-9 :
    1. Industrial productivity--United States--Case studies.
2. Quality control--Statistical methods--Case studies.   3. Deming, W.
Edwards (William Edwards), 1900- .   I. Roome, Diana Reynolds.   II.
Gluckman, Perry, 1938-1992. Everyday heroes. III. Title.
HD56.G58   1993
338 .064 0922--dc20   93-15975
                                                          CIP

Cover Design: Faville Design

All characters and companies portrayed in the stories, except for the historical figures mentioned, are strictly fictional. Any resemblance to actual events is purely coincidental.

Distributed in the United Kingdom, Ireland, Europe, and Africa by John Wiley & Sons Ltd., Chichester, Sussex, England.

Distributed in the English language in Singapore, the Philippines, and southeast Asia by Toppan Co., Ltd., Singapore; and in the English language in Japan by Toppan Co., Ltd., Tokyo, Japan.

Printed in the United States of America

Library of Congress Catalog Number 93-15975
ISBN: 0-932633-26-9   12 11 10 9 8 7 6 5 4 3 2 1

CONTENTS

ACKNOWLEDGMENTS

IF WE WERE TO RECOGNIZE everyone who contributed significantly to this book and to detail their efforts, this section would be longer than the entire book. That being said, we acknowledge the importance of a team effort and appreciate everyone's contribution. We apologize in advance for omitting anyone.

George Watson's extensive consulting experience contributed much to the ideas communicated in this book, and along with Don Wheeler, he contributed to the axioms discussed in the Afterword. His perceptive judgment gave good guidance to all. Marian Hirsch wrote the epilogues to each story and played a major role in editing, preparing, and producing the text. Special appreciation goes to Jay Gluckman for his understanding and cooperation under difficult circumstances. He spent numerous hours typesetting and designing the cover for one edition of the book. Marcia Daszko acted as producer and director of this entire project and kept all participants focused on it. Charles Roome offered insights and ideas as the stories developed. In any project of this nature, certain individuals will pitch in to help whenever and wherever needed. Special thanks go to Dan Robertson and Harriet Hillyer for their exceptional patience and for doing more than was asked.

Many of the ideas expressed in this book are directly or indirectly derived from the works of Lloyd S. Nelson, Ph.D., the Director of Statistical Methods of the Nashua Corporation. He has pioneered novel ways of expressing many of Dr. Deming's ideas. In particular, he developed the use of the funnel demonstration to illustrate the cost of tampering with the system when we treat common causes as special causes. He also coined the phrase "unknown and unknowable," which is often used to express the idea that the information needed for optimizing any system is frequently unavailable through the usual processes. We appreciate his contributions.

We want to acknowledge the more than seventy-five "friendly allies" who entrusted us with their business situations, which enabled us to develop our ideas. The late Jim Farrell, in particular, worked with us for five of the last ten years in three different companies. Much of what is written in this book came out of discussions with him. We and the world have lost a good friend in Jim Farrell.

More than one hundred people read some or all of the text in various stages and gave constructive, well-considered comments. The following people were among the reviewers who gave generously of their time:

Marcia Daszko	Dan Robertson
Jay Gluckman	Stan Myers
Dave Buck	Ken Roerden
Page Shirtum	Sue Sorem
Bill Howell	Bill Boller
Hugh Treanor	Carolyn Shamlin
George Watson	Martha Watson
Bill Harris	Barbara Kent
Jenny Hopkinson	Barry Cioffi
Tim Fuller	E.M. Haschke
Tanya Lee	Lynn Brewer
Kirby Lowery	Mike Moran

PREFACE

WHAT CAN AMERICAN industry do to become more productive? Would companies operate better if they followed the philosophy of W. Edwards Deming? The intent of this book is to answer these questions and to present a clear picture of what is involved in changing our thinking about the way we do business.

Most companies are still run under Frederick Taylor's theories of scientific management, an early twentieth-century approach which is no longer adequate to meet today's challenges. Taylor contributed much by teaching us to develop systems to accomplish repetitive tasks, which in turn helped industry achieve major improvements in productivity and efficiency. Taylor assumed that the systems developed could be optimal.

However, Deming has shown that all systems contain flaws, and that, by using statistical methods to find and remove these flaws, we can continuously improve our systems. Are these ideas really that important to our business operations? Yes. In order to become competitive, companies will have to understand the difference between Taylor's philosophy and Deming's philosophy, and make the needed changes.

The seeds of this book were sown in 1974, when Dr. Sidney Fernbach hired me to apply statistical thinking to the computer center operations at the Lawrence Livermore National Laboratory. The center was having trouble with the reliability of its large computers. (Dr. Fernbach had taken a class from Deming in 1944 and learned that even a large center could be controlled by simple statistical tools applied correctly.)

The methods we used during the next eighteen months closely followed those described by Deming in several of his papers. Not only was computer reliability improved by every measure, but we achieved a return on our investment of over one thousand to one during the first full year. Deming's approach worked, but it was difficult for many people to understand why it worked.

The fifteen years following the Lawrence Livermore events have seen more experiments in improvement, more human experiences with change, and a growing sense of urgency that as many companies and people as possible be exposed to Deming's ideas. The six stories that follow show what happens when theory meets reality. Each epilogue discusses the principles behind the events and reinforces the lessons learned. Here readers will gain a glimpse of the difficulties and rewards of change, and of Deming's philosophy in action.

December 1989   P.G.
Los Altos, California

FOREWORD

A JOB DESCRIPTION must do more than prescribe motions, do this, do that; don't do that. It must explain how the work being done fits into the system; how the item being worked on will be used.

Suppose that you tell me that my job is to wash this table. You hand to me a bucket of hot water, soap, brush, rags. I still have no idea what the table will be used for after I wash it. Is it to be clean enough to eat off? If so, it is clean enough now; a sloppy job will suffice. If it is to be used for an operating table, then a lot of washing would be required—top, bottom, legs; and a second wash, and scalding water.

A programmer said to me that she could do a much better job with fewer mistakes if she knew what the program would be used for. "The specifications don't tell me what I need to know."

A flow diagram of any process will divide the work into stages. Work comes into any stage, changes state, and moves on into the next stage. Every stage has a customer, which is the next stage. The final stage will send product or service to the ultimate customer, he that buys the product or the service. The stages will usually not be individual, independent activities. They should be geared toward optimum performance of the process. The stages as a whole form a process. Every activity, every job, is a part of the process. Everyone on the job needs to understand the aim of the process.

The process must be managed for optimum results for the effort expended. Anyone on a job has responsibility to increase his knowledge of his process. He has an obligation to pass this information along to his coworkers, possibly in writing, so that his accretion of knowledge is not lost when he moves along to another job. It is a loss to society to reinvent the wheel. The syndrome NIH (not invented here) must be replaced by optimization, cooperation.

This book by Perry Gluckman explains in delightful reading the changes that are taking place in leadership. It is a pleasure to express to him my thanks and appreciation for this work.

February 1990   W. Edwards Deming
Washington

INTRODUCTION TO THE SECOND EDITION

THE FIRST TIME I met Perry Gluckman he was bent over, as though he were dizzy or had a stomachache. When he straightened up and I introduced myself, I saw that he was tall, with a van Dyke beard and wild, curly hair. Having read *Everyday Heroes,* I had contacted Perry, and was invited to hear him teach a class for the Bay Area Deming User Group. I got more than I had bargained for.

At this point in my journey into the philosophy of W. Edwards Deming, I had attended two of Deming's four-day seminars, had sat in on his classes at New York University, had traveled with him on a consulting trip, and had exchanged ideas with him frequently by phone and letter. Most of the books written by or about Deming lined my shelves. I considered myself, if not expert, then at least totally familiar with the Deming philosophy.

I was not ready for someone who had *analyzed* both Deming's ideas and their origins, and who, in the course of this intellectual detective work, had discovered the roots of today's management style along with its failings.

That evening's lecture was on the theory of knowledge, one of the four cornerstones of what Deming calls "a system of profound knowledge." Perry had dissected the work of Clarence Lewis, an epistemologist, and Percy Bridgman, a physicist, both of whom had influenced Deming considerably—but not, apparently, one another, even though they had been contemporaries on the Harvard campus.

Perry Gluckman understood the Deming philosophy as few have. His life revolved around a goal: to get Deming's message to as many people as he could, but especially to managers. Perry's own consultancy was the first step; the book in front of you is the second. Instead of regurgitating Deming's own sayings, his life story, or his current work with his clients, *Everyday Heroes* tries to do something new: It compares Deming's philosophy with that of Frederick Taylor, whose scientific management system provided the philosophy for both western and Japanese management in the early part of this century; and it presents the philosophy in a way that almost anyone can understand. For this latter goal, Perry adopted the parable form of teaching.

Of course, a *parable* is a narrative that may be pointed to as an illustration of a principle to follow or avoid. If you read a parable without understanding, you will get no benefit from its message—which is why I recommend that you read each of the six parables in *Everyday Heroes* at least twice, the second time more slowly, asking yourself *why* Perry is saying what he does.

These parables are based on actual experiences, although names of people and companies have been changed. You will be able to see yourself and your colleagues here. By tapping into this immediately recognizable tribal knowledge, Perry evokes validation from you about your own experience. With each thoughtful reading, you can get closer to the level of the principles Perry is teaching.

Perry was a mathematical statistician, not a great literary genius. Everyday life seldom makes great literature—but each of these parables has a hero, someone who does something extraordinary and good, by following sound principles. The pity, of course, is that such acts *are* extraordinary, and it is this discrepancy that Perry set out to correct by bringing out the principles in practical settings.

We are hooked on success stories and winning. Yet there is more chance to learn from a mistake, a failure, if it is understood why one failed. Then, we can do it a better way next time. The people you'll meet in *Everyday Heroes* are not always successful in an organizational sense; but they do not pass up the opportunities that are given them to learn. Because of this, and other personal qualities, each of the heroes in these parables does become an exemplar of behavior to be followed. The last of these parables is clearly autobiographical, establishing a new level of integrity and principles for management consultants to follow.

The stomachache I thought Perry had was later diagnosed as cancer, and the surgery he underwent left him bedridden with less than a year to live. A small group of his friends helped him use that final period of his life to initiate a third project, which would lead to a much fuller account of Deming's philosophy: the writing of the book *Deming's Profound Changes,* of which I am a coauthor. To the end of his life, Perry demonstrated the purposefulness, guts, and persistence that are required from anyone who will transform the people whose very "success" has made them most resistant to improvement: management.

Perry Gluckman was a gentle man and a fine teacher. May his legacy be an effective tool in achieving the transformation we so desperately need. Enjoy this book and learn from it; then share it with a friend—and a manager.

March 1993   Ken Delavigne
Coyote, California

EVERYDAY HEROES
OF THE
QUALITY MOVEMENT

INTRODUCTION

THIS IS A BOOK ABOUT change, and the people who make it happen. There is almost universal agreement among businesses and industry that profound changes are necessary if the United States is to be a top competitor in the world of the future. But what kind of changes are we really after, and how do we achieve them?

Changes in the broad course of human activity usually begin with subtle shifts in perception among a few people whose ideas spread as others come to understand and accept their point of view. Often, changes in perception bring with them a need to alter the way things are done. This process is rather like the tipping of a scale, as a few convince the majority that the new ways are wiser, more humane, or more productive.

The everyday heroes of this book are individuals who begin the tipping of the scales. They are often unsung, and may even risk their livelihood or status to stand out and oppose the old ways. Sometimes, they are unwelcome because they bring the discomfort that is an inevitable part of change. But their persistence is the raw energy that fuels the evolution of the human world. Brilliant theories would remain forever inert without the catalyzing effect of these change-makers: people who have the courage to imagine, and then commit to creating change for a better future, be it in a more civilized attitude or greater productivity.

Heroes of our technological age have little in common, at least on the surface, with heroes of the past. They struggle with forces that are harder to define than poverty or the long, grueling hours in dark offices braved by Horatio Alger's boys. Today's heroes are harder to identify than the colorful heroes of legend who fought dragons or the forces of evil. Most will never have their stories told. Yet they often tackle forces just as difficult and dangerous: ignorance, fear, egotism, tradition, and inertia. Instead of a universe of demons and princesses, they inhabit a world where ideas and technologies are gaining ascendance over those of property, capital, and physical might.

The protagonists of these six stories have little in common except their conviction (sometimes sorely challenged) about an idea that they believe can transform the processes and people around them. They range from a production assembler who persists in questioning the status quo, to a chief executive who tries to convey and implement a new concept of managing. Their stories vary in difficulty reflecting the central character's level of awareness.

Change is often achieved at the cost of great personal pain and difficulty. Some characters find themselves pursuing a mission they may not want, or for which they do not feel suited. But in taking on the challenge, they assume leadership and help to redirect the course of human effort. Although they may see their struggles as personal ones, they are actually part of a much larger and more significant evolution that is taking place throughout American industry and beyond.

Like major shifts of the past, this present evolution is affecting the way we think about everything in business. Society changed subtly but profoundly as Newton's ideas superseded those of Ptolemy in the seventeenth century. Newtonian physics supposed that the world around us was as deterministic as a good Swiss clock. It proposed a computable and measurable relation between what was happening now, and what had happened at any time in the past. Furthermore, this chain of action and reaction could be projected into the future. For two centuries, our entire worldview was based on this assumption of causal relationships.

This all changed in the twentieth century, with the introduction of quantum physics. Quantum mechanics, which baffles many experts and even perplexed Einstein himself, is still causing upheavals in the way society functions, although we are often unaware of them. Quantum physics tell us that relationships between events may be nonlinear and impossible to predict. Little has been left untouched by these revolutionary ideas, and the material world of manufacturing is no exception.

Until recently, many systems of production developed under modes of thought dominated by Newtonian physics were assumed to be optimal. The only flaws that were recognized were those arising from people not understanding or following procedures, from improper supervision, or poor motivation.

In the light of twentieth century physics, certain statisticians, Dr. Walter Shewhart and Dr. W. Edwards Deming among them, began to think about systems in new ways. Deming understood that the information needed to set up optimal systems is unknown and unknowable. He recognized that there is an entirely different category of flaws, which have nothing to do with human performance, although they are often attributed to workers. This causes much negative feeling and little positive improvement.

The flaws are built into a system because of randomness, and are a great deal harder to pinpoint because they are not localized in time and space. These variations cannot be predicted, as Newtonian physics would have taught us. They are present in every system, and it is the job of those who are interested in process improvement to understand the dynamics of these built-in flaws and to remove them.

Deming said that by removing the built-in flaws in the manufacturing systems that we have, we can incrementally and continuously improve our organizations. Only by this route will we realize the potential of our nation's enormous energy, brain power, and inventiveness.

The characters portrayed here demonstrate what can happen when we apply our present understanding and our energies to continuous process improvement. The change in emphasis, from people to systems, can have dramatic effects on people's lives and on their companies' productivity. Removing the built-in flaws that cause complexity releases energy at many levels. Many of the numerical results quoted in this book may appear incredible, but companies have actually experienced these improvements.

These stories are distilled from the experience of working in organizations and with people who have attempted to change from the old ways to the new. The characters experience the turmoil that comes with such change. They also begin to explore new ways of thinking, which can alter our assumptions about organization and efficiency.

The stories are about all of us. Readers who have the capacity to create change should find their own story reflected in one, if not more, of them. We hope the fortitude and persistence of our heroes will give readers encouragement in forging their own way ahead, in the knowledge that their efforts are understood, at least by a few.

And if such simple ego-fodder is not enough, this book also reflects what we have found to be true: When a company puts itself on the road to change and continuous improvement, the gains can be truly awesome.

1

THE MANAGER'S STORY
A Matter of Fortitude

TURNING INTO THE company parking lot, Wanda Carroll narrowly missed a dark blue car coming out. Her right tire bumped over the curb, hitting the wheel of her new Honda Prelude. She could feel her blood pressure rising, and the day hadn't even started yet. "Oh, great!" she muttered aloud. "Bad judgment seems to be my disease these days."

Wanda was due to undergo the semiannual ordeal of her performance review and she had a nasty suspicion that it would not be enjoyable. Since her arrival at Garrison Electronics almost two years before, Wanda had achieved things that sometimes amazed even her. As production manager of an analog board assembly plant, she had first set about getting rid of the shortages which had long strangled productivity. She worked with suppliers to help them solve their problems until they were all delivering on time.

Assembly cycle times started to speed up as Wanda maneuvered a "pull" system of material flow into place. She had coaxed workers with a vision of what could be achieved, repeatedly showing them how to make improvements and encouraging them to think of ways to get their own areas running more smoothly. Empty space appeared, as stacks of incomplete orders became things of the past. The assembly area, where circuit boards were put together for the company's line of car radios, looked as orderly as a parade ground.

Many improvements had come in the last seven months. A seventy-five percent reduction in the standard cost for each unit was reflected in the product cost to the consumer, and orders increased threefold. The analog board plant, once plagued by shortages and bottlenecks, was now operating like a model plant. It ran without serious hitches and was equal to the increased demand.

The changes were like magic. Wanda now understood why the wizard in her favorite Disney movie got so cranky after casting spells. Transformation is never easy. But when it is done well, it has a way of looking obvious to everyone else. After the magic spell was cast on the chaotic castle kitchen and the rebellious crockery stood once again in ordered ranks, it looked like nothing out of the ordinary. But what effort the old wizard had put into that whirlpool of reorganization!

Wanda was the only person who had any idea of the work that had gone into streamlining her department, except perhaps Dave Rollo, her old division manager. Not that she minded. She was only too glad that her spell had worked. But there was a problem. Nobody outside her department seemed to have noticed the vast improvement.

Orders poured in and costs plummeted. But nobody—neither the manufacturing manager nor any of the production managers from other divisions—had said a word. If anything, her work seemed to cause suspicion among her peers and superiors.

It would be easy enough to attribute the lack of recognition to the fact that she was a female operating successfully in the traditionally male preserve of manufacturing. No doubt that did cause consternation to some. But it was more than that: The uneasiness was caused by the fact that most people simply failed to understand what she was doing, and even more, why she was doing it.

The hang-up was the curious fact that Wanda's department, while operating better and better, was at the same time getting smaller and smaller. In many people's opinions, to reduce one's empire went against the laws of nature. Surely, for any self-respecting manager, bigger was always better.

Now she was due to be judged: Was Wanda's department a success or was it simply an anomaly?

Entering the lobby, where the smell of new carpeting assailed her nose, Wanda practically had another collision. But this time it was not her fault. Jake Dempster, the quality manager, was storming out the door as if something had bitten him. He threw Wanda a poisonous look before pushing past her without a greeting or apology.

Wanda walked briskly up the corridor to her own department, where the assembly was already well underway for the day. Just inside the door, she was greeted by the department supervisor, Alan, who was clearly on the lookout for her.

"Wanda, there's been a real stink with Jake Dempster. He's just been in here demanding to see our figures. I don't think he believes what we say about the increase in productivity. He's also very worried that our defect rate will go up now that Susan has moved out. He absolutely won't believe it's stayed stable."

Wanda groaned inwardly. Getting good results sometimes seemed to cause more problems than getting bad ones. "How's the problem with the solder?" she asked.

"Not too bad," replied Alan. "We're setting up the temperature gauge charts now. I have a hunch it's a fluctuation in the temperature that's causing that glitch."

As she listened, Wanda realized that she was trembling. Her review was at eleven o'clock with Irwin Shaw, the manufacturing manager of four months standing. Since his arrival, she had received very little support. In fact, he had all but ignored her and her department, as if they were too small or insignificant to bother about.

To make things worse, Irwin was a good friend of Jake Dempster's. Jake had worked at Irwin's previous company. She knew they played golf together at the new golf course a couple of miles away. Their wives were friendly, too. Wanda couldn't help wondering what Jake had been saying about her as he strolled down the green to the next hole.

Having once been quite hearty in his encouragement of her efforts, sometimes even congratulatory, Jake's behavior had gradually grown icy. She saw less of him now because her department's defect rates had taken a plunge. Jake was hardly necessary anymore. Wanda knew where their few remaining defects were coming from, because of the careful monitoring they were doing on most of their processes. Where there was a problem, they were tackling it, quite successfully in most cases.

She wished Dave Rollo were still here. Most of the changes in her department had happened under Dave's watchful but trusting eye, until he left to follow his wife's career to another part of the country. As previous division manager, Dave had taught her a lot. What she learned in theory Dave helped her put into practice.

Wanda was sorry to see him go. But losing her major source of encouragement did not stop her from taking a stand. She found herself hooked on the idea of achieving better productivity scores, in the same way that a sportsman gets hooked on scores in football or baseball. She applied herself to the task of learning more about the theory and practice of different quality improvement techniques. She even turned down dates to attend classes.

Although friends laughed incredulously at her dedication, at night she would lie in bed redesigning production areas in the same way a painter plays with the canvas in her imagination.

"You carry on with the charts," said Wanda to Alan. "I've got the figures Jake wants."

In her office, she pulled out the charts showing measurements of cycle times, defects, and products shipped. Even in her anxiety, she could not help feeling a flush of pride. Parts shortages had slid from one hundred twenty-five per day to less than five, in the space of six months. Scrap had plummeted, and now stood at less than one percent. Returns stood at an all-time low of half a percentage point. And to top it all, productivity was up forty percent.

As she started entering the figures, Wanda wondered whether even these would carry the same weight in Shaw's mind as a few offhand remarks on the golf course. She could hear the kind of thing: "Wanda's a plucky gal, taking on Just-in-Time single-handedly. But she thinks it all works like clockwork. Doesn't realize that eighty percent of all JIT programs fail in this country. The Japanese may have the trick, but it's not our way. Why should she succeed where so many other people have failed?"

Then another voice: "And look at her department. People leaving in droves. That department was twenty-three strong when she came into it. Look at it now. I think there are about twelve left. Does she want to economize away the entire company?"

It was true. Jobs had been evaporating. Nobody had been fired, but as problems were tackled and solved, fewer people were needed to deal with them. For example, as the problem of shortages dwindled, the expediter's job became unnecessary. Bob, the warehouse manager, had moved over to another department because there was nothing to warehouse anymore. Parts were received and assembled boards were quickly moved to upper-level assembly. There were no pileups of boards requiring a recheck, rework, or the insertion of missing parts.

Alan, who had been in charge of rework on the production line, was promoted to supervisor and nobody was brought in to replace him in his old job. The department had dwindled to almost half its old size. Even the floor area had grown as clutter receded. By mutual agreement, the space was taken over and used by the company's digital board assembly plant, to store their incomplete boards awaiting parts.

Susan was the latest person to go. She was no longer needed to inspect boards and check orders before they went out. Accuracy had rocketed and remained so stable that her job was superfluous, and she was bored.

The demise of Susan's job was important. It meant a major shift in the way the department worked and it also helped to explain Jake Dempster's visitation and hasty exit that morning. Instead of sending each completed board off to a final inspection (done by Susan, supervised by Jake), each worker had to keep an eagle eye on his or her own performance. It was not just idealism that kept them improving. What made it all work were the charts. Everyone kept records, and these were posted.

This was not an expose-the-evildoers routine, as people were not publicly castigated if they slipped. Just seeing a downward curve in their own chart seemed to do the trick, without a supervisor or manager saying a word. People got almost instant feedback on their own performance as the charts were filled in every day.

It was like playing a game, each trying to outdo his own best record. If simply trying harder didn't improve a score, a worker would turn to Alan or Wanda for help in tracking down the culprit, which usually turned out to be a flaw in the system. This technique worked so well that Susan had been able to move, thankfully, as it turned out, to a new job in the personnel department.

Looking at her watch, Wanda realized that she would have to stop reviewing the progress of events in her department, and act fast. She was not one to go around justifying herself. Up to now, she had assumed that the results of her work were evidence enough of her skills. But Jake's strange behavior this morning, and now his demand for evidence on paper, made it very clear that they were not. If that was the case, she would have to be her own advocate, and a good one at that.

She phoned through to the department supervisor. "Alan, I have to spend half an hour or so in my office. D'you mind completing those charts yourself? I'll take a look at them later."

Finding her Rolodex, she started leafing through it as fast as she could. "Calder . . . Cosel . . . Cosek!" Yes—that was it! Several months ago, Wanda had attended a seminar in Los Angeles about implementing Just-in-Time systems. The company had sponsored her participation with some reluctance. At coffee after lunch on the second day, she met a consultant who was there to give a talk on the uses of statistics in implementing Just-in-Time.

This man, Stanley Cosek, was a friend of W. Edwards Deming, the celebrated guru of process control who had done so much to help the Japanese economy get back on its feet after World War II.

Cosek, who was refreshingly lacking in pretension, told Wanda he was also there to observe. "I am a consultant on a treasure hunt," he said with a smile. "I'm trying to understand why people are failing to implement JIT in this country. I have a feeling that if they would use statistics the way the Japanese do, they would get far better results."

Wanda realized she had been offered a rare chance to pick an exceptional brain, and at the same time, offer something back by telling the story of her own department. Later that day, she described her own progress, and the areas where she was not doing so well. In return, Cosek told her how he had worked with a large U.S. company to reduce defects and decrease cycle times in one of its computer manufacturing plants. By the end, she felt the way she imagined an eye surgeon would have felt on first hearing about the laser. She knew she was on the verge of discovering a new tool of tremendous power and importance.

"Most people who want to get JIT going take the whole system apart and redesign it. But, as often as not, they design in a whole new set of flaws. We see a much simpler, less costly way to do it, which works better too. We reduce complexity in the system. We reduce the built-in flaws, using statistics to measure and track them until they're all gone. Then, presto! you can implement JIT. It's pure logic."

Cosek gave a practiced flourish to his hand as he ended his small speech. "I used to do magic tricks when I was a boy," he confided with a mischievous grin. "I suppose this job is just a more grown-up way of doing magic."

Before leaving the seminar, Cosek came up to Wanda and took her by the arm. "I don't want you to think implementing SQC and JIT is like waving a wand, even though I joked about the magic," he said. "There's nothing instant about what I advocate. It takes work and commitment. People often don't understand it. Maybe you'll try it one day. You look like a lady of courage."

Wanda had been flattered by the compliment. She had gone home and read about Deming and his extraordinary achievements in Japan, and more recently with such companies as Ford in the U.S.A. She had used her new knowledge wherever she could, and had often thought back to the guidelines Cosek gave at the seminar.

But now, what kept echoing in her mind was something he had said, though she had not given it a second thought at the time: "People often don't understand it."   She decided she would have to talk to Cosek—now.

Miraculously, he was in. "I remember you," he said. "I'd be glad to help, though I have to go out in about half an hour."

"I'll be as brief as I can," said Wanda, trying not to sound breathless. She could hardly believe her luck. Even ten minutes of conversation with a person who understood what she was trying to do sounded as good as winning the lottery. "I have my review later this morning," she said, remembering her own time constraints.

"Ah, the human lottery," commented Cosek with a short laugh, picking up on her thought in a way she had noticed when she met him. "That's all part of the madness of today's management style in this country. Reward the ones that make the most noise; ignore or punish the ones that quietly get things done. From what you told me, I expect the second reaction is what you'll get."

Wanda took a deep breath of relief. Even at this distance and with this little acquaintance, she felt the immediate sense of revelation and confirmation that comes from tuning in on someone else's wavelength, and getting perfect reception. She felt she was not only understanding with clarity and precision, but that she also was being perceived and understood. Compared to the response from her company, hearing Cosek was like listening to a digital recording after ordinary stereo.

"Yes, but if I'm punished, what good will that do the department? We've worked hard to come this far. I don't want all that effort to be undone, just so that the traditional forms can be kept up." Wanda briefly explained what had happened: the reductions in the size of the department, the production and defect figures that were not always believed, and the quality manager's alarmed reaction.

Cosek listened in silence, then said, "People don't always understand that a simple, flawless system is a work of art. What they see is that you seem to be less busy, and are in control of fewer people. This makes you look as if you're doing less, working less hard. Ultimately, it makes you look less important."

"But surely," Wanda said, "it must be obvious what I've

tried to achieve and that the reductions will save the company a whole lot of expense?"

"If you were in control of a department which was full of complexity and always visible because of repeated crises, where people were at each other's throats, and if you had to bring in more people to be able to cope, then people would see you as a powerful, busy person. And you would be expanding your empire nicely. And if you could keep all that mess in line, then you'd be seen as a great manager. People would understand that perfectly." Cosek let out a short laugh of genuine merriment at his own pessimistic picture.

Wanda did not join in. His description had an almost macabre accuracy to it. But the other side of the truth was that while there were no crises in Wanda's department, there was a big crisis for her self-esteem. It was all very well keeping one's ego out of the work place, but was it too much to ask to have one's achievements at least acknowledged? Being reviled for them seemed a little beyond the pale.

"It's good to hear you say all that, Mr. Cosek. But how do I convince them of it at my review? I don't think I'm up to re-educating this large company single-handedly."

"You're not doing it single-handedly. I'm helping you."

"But what do I do?" Wanda was beginning to hear a wail in her voice, as if she were a small girl again. Normally smart, self-confident, and completely in control, she suddenly felt unable to believe in herself, let alone act as her own advocate.

"Wanda," said Cosek, and his voice suddenly seemed much nearer. "You're falling into the helplessness trap. Don't do it. That's exactly what has happened too much in American industry. People don't think they can change things. They don't think they can affect our slide downhill, so they let the avalanche gather speed. Helplessness is a form of sickness. Aborigines in Australia have died from it when the witch doctor pointed a bone at them. Don't let anyone point a bone at you. You have proven that you are far from being a helpless person. You have strength and will, and you have already made great changes. The worst is behind you. Now all you have to do is show them what you've done. You just have to have fortitude."

As Wanda listened, she felt her sense of purpose begin to flow back. She realized she had been sitting slumped over her desk, with her head on her hand as she spoke. Now she straightened up, her belief in herself almost restored.

"I think you've convinced me, Mr. Cosek. I'm still nervous, but I don't think I'm going to let them crush me like a fly. In fact, I may have a thing or two to teach them."

Cosek laughed. "Call me if you need help again," he said warmly. "I have a vested interest in improving American industry, you know. I happen to think quite highly of this country, but at the moment we're heading for a crisis equal to the fall of Rome. You can be one of my generals and help prevent the invasion of the mediocre. Good luck."

***

Approaching Shaw's door at two minutes to eleven that morning, Wanda repeated to herself a word that was beginning to sound almost like a mantra: "Fortitude."

It helped, but not enough. Her premonition that the meeting would be discouraging would not go away. Shaw gave her his professional smile as she entered, and waved her into the leather chair in front of his desk.

"Well, Wanda, how're you doing?" came the formula greeting, followed by a brief laugh before the inevitable: "Keeping the boys in line, as usual?"

Shaw's patronizing references to her age and sex always infuriated Wanda, especially when they implied the kind of coercive relationship between manager and workers that she deliberately discouraged.

"I think the people in our department are quite able to keep themselves in order, Irwin," she replied, making an effort to keep her voice even. "I've been impressed by the high quality of their work."

As she spoke, she heard her real answer bubbling inside her head: "I'm worried sick, and furious with you for putting me through this charade. I'm a good manager and you can't even see it. The stereotypes in your head are so immovable that there's not enough room for any real consideration of what's going on."

She wondered, as she held back her real feelings, why her early training in good manners remained so effective. On top of this, the obligatory masking of nasty news with a good-natured joke was a convention she despised.

Shaw started with a litany of statistics and figures. They were the figures for her department, compared with those for a couple of other assembly areas, including the one she thought of as her twin: Jim Willens' department, P13, which did an almost identical job to her own. As she listened, Wanda realized that her department sounded puny and insignificant compared to the others. It was supremely ironic that everything she had worked for during the past year and a half had boiled down to a list of numbers that proved her a small manager in a dwindling department.

This was the scenario that started to emerge: By reducing standard costs so drastically, her products could be offered at a lower price to other departments that bought them. Sales were climbing because the price reduction had been passed on to the customer. But—here was the crunch—Wanda's department was now making less profit because it was producing so cheaply. Looked at in isolation, the figures looked paltry. The increased sales and profits to the company were not recorded in such a way that they could be attributed to Wanda's choreographing of her department into a tight-knit and highly efficient organization.

She heard Shaw saying, "We think you've done a good job, Wanda, and your department has achieved some excellent results, especially in the areas of cutting down on rework, and reducing cycle times. But given the size of your department and our company's need to reduce costs, we've decided to combine your section with the assembly department P13."

Wanda's head began to feel like a helium balloon. The hope that this might mean a promotion battled with the more likely probability that her work would be passed over as something achieved so elegantly simply because it was so easy to do in the first place.

"Jim Willens, who manages P13, has had a good deal more experience than you. His department is larger, and he's managing a more complex situation. Merging the two departments will take someone who has worked with a difficult situation before. We hope you two will be able to work together, because your knowledge of your own area will be invaluable to Jim."

He looked at her to gauge her reaction for a moment, then went on without pausing as he saw her spine stiffen and her eyes narrow. "In effect, this will be a promotion, Wanda," he said with a note of apology in his voice. "You will still be production manager but you'll have other first-level managers reporting to you. You'll report to Jim Willens, who will remain production manager of the combined departments. This will be more a matter of formality than anything else. You and Jim will be working as a combined powerhouse, as it were." He cleared his throat uneasily.

Wanda decided to take the plunge. "Mr. Shaw," she said, "I'd like to point out that the size of my department, and its profitability on paper, is no reflection on its effectiveness. Taking the figures as a whole, we have actually been more productive than P13, with less staff and fewer resources. Our profits have only gone down because our unit costs have gone down and we've passed on that advantage. You must see that it's done the company nothing but good. The way the metrics are designed are skewed. . . ."

Wanda started to feel herself failing. It was almost as if company structure, like a terrible, formless monster, had become her opponent. Gathering her arguments, she began again.

"Maybe we should ask ourselves, What is our measure of success? Are we interested only in high numbers, regardless of what they mean, or their significance to the whole company? And the size of the department is exactly what I planned for P14. I deliberately reduced the floor area and positions so that we could bring down the complexity. There were too many unnecessary activities going on before and they only offered more opportunities for things to go wrong.

"This kind of linearization was the right thing to do if I was to implement JIT successfully. If you will look at our figures again, you'll see that our productivity has gone up threefold over the past six months, and our costs are down by seventy-five percent. I don't want to sound carping, but P13's productivity has fluctuated and is now half a percentage point above what it was six months ago."

She saw Shaw's eyes shift downward as he tried to hide his irritation—or was it embarrassment? His reply came after a moment in which he tried to muster his argument. "Jim's department has struggled with some unusual difficulties this year," he said. "He's had trouble with vendors and big design problems with some parts. That accounts for the productivity figures."

Wanda's reply came fast. "We had trouble with suppliers too, nine months ago. We solved them all. Our backorders were much like Jim's when I first came, but we worked with our suppliers, one by one, and we have no shortages now."

For a moment, a flicker of surprise registered in Shaw's eyes. It was clear that he had not realized there were problems worth solving in P14.

"Good, good," he said evenly. "I like to hear stories like that."

When he did not ask how she had done it, Wanda decided to volunteer the information anyhow. It was important that Shaw realize what tremendous changes had come about. "We used statistics, Pareto charts, and Shewhart control charts to find out exactly what was causing the holdups. It was a number of things, of course; sometimes our fault, sometimes the suppliers' faults. But the data gave us something to work on. When we showed the suppliers the charts, they knew we were not being unreasonable. It was amazing how willing they were to work with us."

It was clear now that Shaw was beginning to listen. He asked Wanda a few more questions: Where else had she set up the charts? How did the workers respond to the extra bother of keeping them current? How was her department keeping track of finished goods if she was getting rid of quality inspectors and procedures?

Twenty minutes later, Wanda walked out of Shaw's office

with a little more hope that he now understood why her department was shrinking. She had done her best to explain that it was getting smaller not because it had failed but because it was succeeding. In a nutshell, it was doing more with less. If Shaw had time to think about what she had told him, there was a chance he might reconsider his decision.

But a week later, a written confirmation of the merger of the two departments dashed her hopes. Either Shaw had not wanted to understand the significance of her accomplishments, or he did not have the guts to change his earlier decision, in light of what he had learned.

Not long afterwards, Wanda found herself talking to Abe Manlow, vice president of manufacturing, at a meeting of the local chapter of an electronics quality organization. She had seen him at a meeting some weeks ago when the subject of using statistical data for long-term quality control had been discussed. He was a pleasant fellow, due to retire in a few months, and she decided she would lose nothing by asking him about the fate of her department—and herself.

As she approached, Manlow addressed her with a welcoming smile: "Hello, Wanda. I'm sorry to hear about the demise of your department." Seeing her expression and being a person of tact, Manlow quickly qualified his remark. "Well, it's not a demise, I know. It'll be a regeneration with all the strength of P13 to back it up."

Clearly, it was too late. The failure to understand what she had done in her department was endemic. If the VP of manufacturing failed to grasp the significance of her work, there was little hope of anyone else in the company understanding either, aside from the people she worked with directly, bless them.

The meeting was nearing an end, but she decided to hold on to her fortitude and let him know as much about what she had achieved as she could in the time available. With his head inclined slightly, Manlow listened to her story. His expression was conciliatory, even sympathetic.

When she had finished, he said "Wanda, I'm impressed with what you've just told me, and with your clear grasp of the real meaning of quality. But I think you have a problem: not in your work or your department, but in communication. People are just not ready to understand these ideas. When somebody comes and tells them that they should do something which seems to contradict everything they've known before, they see no reason why they should go along with it. They would rather find an instant answer to their productivity problems, something that doesn't rock the boat or challenge anyone too much.

"I'm with you. I would very much like to implement the kinds of ideas you're talking about throughout the company. But it will take time. It's a tragedy, really. I wish I could have done more to make things different."

Manlow sighed, and looked at the door where people were gathering to say their goodbyes and leave the meeting.

Wanda took a last plunge. If Manlow had given up on the company, at least she wanted to find out where she stood in it. "Mr. Manlow, I really am confused. If P14 and P13 merge, where does this leave me?"

Manlow looked thoughtful. "I have to be honest with you, Wanda, as you're clearly a person of integrity and purpose. The best you can do is to look for another position in the company."

"But all the work that's gone into streamlining our department—all that headway will be lost." Wanda felt rotten about the doors that kept closing on her. But she felt even worse at the thought of her department slipping back into its old habits: backlogs, missing parts, defects, and missed delivery dates.

"It's sad," Manlow's face was turned toward the door again. She could see he wanted to leave. "You're ahead of your time, Wanda, like myself. I understand what you're trying to do because I tried too. Our corporations are not ready for these kinds of changes yet. It takes education, and a commitment from everyone. I wish I could sound more hopeful. I'll do my best to put your case to Shaw. And now I must leave. My wife worries about me if I stay out too late."

With a limp handshake and a kind smile, Wanda's best hope walked slowly toward the door.

***

Sometimes when people think they have been pushed to the edge of their endurance, they find they can nudge themselves on a little further. Wanda did consider leaving Garrison. The management's failure to understand her contribution hurt and infuriated her. But she refused to regard her achievements as a lost cause. As long as she continued to believe in them, there was hope that she might be able to gain the same kinds of results again. And if they were ignored a second time, at least she would have the satisfaction of knowing she had done the best work she knew how to do.

Slowly, and with as much patience as she could muster, she tried to apply some of her ideas to running the big combined division. Jim Willens was wedded to traditional ideas of cost accounting efficiencies. Cutting costs was his chief aim, and this meant he was always at odds with his workers, trying to find ways of extracting the most out of them for as little as possible in return. He also liked to think big. He sent huge batches through the production line, and at some point, most of them would get fouled up and lie becalmed, causing backups and frustration all down the line.

From experience in her own department, Wanda knew that many of Jim's theories were sacred cows that had been blocking the traffic of American industry for too long. He sincerely wanted his department to do well, but he could not think beyond what he had been taught.

It was almost impossible to change an old habit by persuasion. But by choosing a few small areas that could benefit from reduced complexity, Wanda tried to demonstrate it by example. When she found her ideas in conflict with Jim's, she tried to back down graciously, and watch the continuing saga of chaos without making her frustration too obvious.

Her own people, already trained in methods of linearity, helped some of the other workers to identify small things they could do to improve the situation, though piecemeal efforts like this often came to nothing.

After enduring the situation for six months, Wanda got an unexpected call from Irwin Shaw to visit him in his office. His voice was cheery, though this, she knew, did not necessarily mean cheerful news for her. But she was wrong. Shaw kept his tasteless jokes to a minimum and went straight to the point.

"We're having a lot of trouble in division K7, which does refinishing and painting of sheet metal over on Avery Road. The scrap rate over there is rocketing, and nobody seems to understand what's causing the problem."

Wanda listened to this confidence and tried to keep her level of astonishment down. It was hard to believe that Shaw would be telling her this if he was not interested in involving her.

"I was talking to Abe Manlow about it yesterday, and he suggested we might give you a chance to try your hand at the situation. It seems he has a lot of confidence in you."

Wanda tried to control her smile, which was threatening to wrap itself right around her face. Now that she was at last being treated as a responsible person, she wanted to behave like a child: to jump on Shaw's desk and shout at the top of her voice.

But her voice was steady when she replied, "I'd be very glad to do whatever I can, Mr. Shaw. When would you like me to start?"

Shaw got out some figures and started to explain the situation to her. It seemed things were so bad in K7 that they were willing to let her try to solve the problems in her own way. They reasoned that nothing could make it worse than it was. She was to start as soon as the supervisor from her old department, Alan, had been primed to take over her job. This was not a difficult matter, as they had worked closely together and thought along similar lines. She hardly envied Alan the honor, though. It was a suffocating situation to be in. But maybe he would find a way of prevailing on Jim to make essential changes in the combined division. It might turn out to be an opportunity for all three of them.

As they talked, Wanda realized that Shaw's tone was not as patronizing as it had been at their previous interview. His questions seemed to indicate a new awareness of what she had achieved in the disbanded analog board department half a year earlier. She wondered if he had learned something by observing the stop-and-start behavior of the new combined division. Maybe he had studied the figures from her department with more care. Or perhaps Manlow had been explaining a thing or two.

When Wanda walked out of Shaw's office, and later on as she thought about her new opportunity, she realized two things. She had been saved from oblivion, it seemed, and given another chance. But this time she would make sure that people better understood what she was doing. Maybe their lack of reaction to her work was not as pigheaded as she had supposed. Maybe they had been genuinely confused, and put her achievements down to luck or an easy situation.

Secondly, she saw that ego played a big part in the workings of the typical American company. Managers who did not advertise their successes were perceived as strange, maybe even threatening in some obscure way. Bragging, even subtly, was an important part of the ritual of survival: so important that it had become part of its substance, too. Managers who did not play an ego-game were in danger of being ignored or even ousted, like the less aggressive males in packs of gorillas.

Wanda had serious doubts that she could ever resemble a male gorilla, but she felt stronger in other ways. Over the months, her work with the sheet metal division gained results similar in magnitude to those in the analog board plant. And to her surprise, "gorilla" tactics were hardly necessary to advertise them. This time the company was on the lookout for results and recognized them when they came.

***

LESSONS FROM THE MANAGER'S STORY

Wanda's Unappreciated Accomplishments

This chapter demonstrates that company leaders who introduce new ideas will probably not be welcomed, and may even encounter resistance. Many readers will recognize their own experiences in the difficulties Wanda suffers. For the sake of American industry, valuable people like her must keep trying to educate others about how the new approach yields continuous improvements.

Until Wanda's arrival, the system at the Garrison Electronics analog board assembly plant was full of complexity, exemplified by people working around missing parts when there were shortages. Some of the problems with suppliers turned out to be due to Garrison's own problems. Wanda's patient work with the suppliers, as well as her instituting a "pull" system, reduces complexity and shortens cycle times immensely.

Wanda's efforts are directed toward controlling and balancing material flow. She works to implement a Just-in-Time system, which controls the logistics of receiving and inventorying materials. By having suppliers reliably deliver smaller lots of parts, inventory can be reduced. The same kind of flow is implemented between work centers in the department as material is "pulled" as needed through the system. Assembly cycle times can be reduced because there is less waiting for parts and the assemblers avoid working around missing parts.

As its standard costs come down, Wanda's department passes along the savings to the next department in line. Ultimately, the cost of the finished product plummets, and customers increase their orders threefold. The control charts kept by each member of Wanda's department have taught them to look first at the system when problems occur. The employees know they are doing the best they can, and they use the charts to get instant feedback on the quality of their work. They need no other external motivation to do good work. Even quality inspection becomes redundant because people are responsible for their own quality assurance.

> **For Discussion:** Compare and contrast Wanda's department with Jim Willens' P13 group.
> ✓ What methods does Jim use?
> ✓ What is important to him?
> ✓ What results does he achieve?

Perception versus Reality

Ironically, Wanda's accomplishments cause her problems. First, as things get better, the department runs smoother. With no crises to focus on, Wanda's supervisors either fail to understand that anything at all has happened, or become suspicious of her actions and motives.

Conspicuous management of crises often gets more recognition than the kind of management that prevents crises in the first place. And, Wanda's accomplishments put crisis management in a different light. Jake Dempster, the quality manager, feels particularly threatened because the department performance indicates that his function has become unnecessary in P14.

Wanda is ultimately hurt by the misperception of what a "successful" department is and does. This often occurs in American corporations. People are suspicious of "pull" systems, and other techniques used by the Japanese, because they believe these methods cannot work in the American cultural milieu. Irwin Shaw wonders what Wanda's "trick" is.

Many people who try to implement JIT in American companies do it without using statistics, or removing complexity from the system. Introducing this new technique to a system burdened with complexity is bound to cause more flaws to appear, and JIT is often blamed as the culprit.

Worst of all, Wanda's department is losing people, and

income is down. While these are actually signs of success (increased volume and lower costs account for the income decline, and the entire company's profits go up), this does not "square" with most managers' concept of a successful department. In addition, the way the company's accounting system is structured, people focus on narrow sets of numbers showing short-term results. The figures for the company's success are not correlated with the performance of Wanda's department.

As Stanley Cosek predicts, despite her attempts to explain what she has done and Mr. Shaw's "motivational" speech, Wanda is essentially punished for all her contributions to Garrison's success.

For Discussion:

✓ What is wrong with the ways Garrison Electronics measures its financial performance?

✓ Where does the company go wrong in evaluating its employees?

Leadership Is No Picnic

In American companies, many people want to be managers because these careers promise power, rewards, and recognition. Wanda is a different sort of manager, and initially she ends up receiving no "perks." Wanda is a true leader. She has the rare ability to impart a vision to her department of how things could be. Unfortunately, she has difficulty imparting this vision to her peers and superiors, partly because she does not seek aggrandizement, and partly because people are resistant.

As Stanley Cosek explains, leadership can be lonely. A simple system is like a work of art, and people may think the manager is doing less. However, despite the risk of being punished, Wanda heeds Cosek's advice to try to maintain her fortitude and to remember that she is not helpless. Wanda cannot afford to give up: If she loses her vision of change, it will never happen. She eventually finds an ally in Abe Manlow, who helps her understand people's resistance to new ideas, and stresses that the problem is not her work, but the incredible challenge of communicating her ideas.

Wanda could leave Garrison, but she decides to stay and contribute where she can. Her opportunity comes with a desperate situation in K7. Things are so bad that Mr. Shaw and the others no longer care about "strange" methods. They are willing to try anything to get results, so Wanda gets free rein. Not every story ends as happily as this one, but leaders should persist. If the situation becomes serious enough, they may be called upon to use the power of their vision.

Wanda must maintain a delicate balance in exercising her leadership. She demonstrates this by working for the company's best interests as opposed to those of any department, group, or individual. However, given the reality of the typical company environment, she must also take steps to ensure her survival. Wanda can do this by making people aware of her activities and helping them understand why she does what she does.

In the ideal corporation, there would be little or no discrepancy between acting in one's self interest and acting in the company's interest. The employees' and the business' interest are congruent. Until this actually happens, people trying to make changes will have to juggle the conflicting demands of management and leadership.

For Discussion:

✓ What do you believe the responsibilities and obligations of a leader are to company management?

✓ What should people do if they disagree with a management decision?

2

THE BUYER'S STORY
No More Deals

TEACH THE SYSTEM the best way to go and then trust it, he thought, as he looked back at one of the most notorious slopes anywhere in Tahoe. Dan Gostler had been a champion skier in his younger days, with a body organized down to the last flinch. It still knew how to make almost any maneuver necessary. All he had to do was let it go.

Gary and Pauline catapulted off the slope and surrounded him, steaming and exhilarated. "Who said you'd forgotten!" shouted Pauline, slapping him on the back. "We saw you!"

Dan beamed. "I dunno. It's been an awful lot of years. I think I'll do a slow one now. Better not push my luck too hard!"

Gliding toward the lifts, Dan felt a new kind of strength flooding him. It wasn't just physical. That one successful descent had somehow given a different meaning to all the mess of the past year. Swinging upward in the chair lift, with Lake Tahoe appearing from under its fringe of trees like a deep blue eye, he felt his confidence returning.

At the summit, Gary and Pauline approached the bump leading to the big slope and disappeared over the top in a cloud of feathery snow. Dan tacked toward the scattering of pines that welcomed skiers who wished to meander. There was a lot on his mind, but it no longer felt like a load of heavy baggage. He could finally think about everything, without feeling impossibly weighed down.

He was no longer missing Joanna, he realized with interest, even though her absence was emphasized with every joke Gary and Pauline shared, and with every look they gave each other. They had skillfully kept their romance a secret from him while they were all working as senior buyers in the purchasing department at Rollins, Inc., manufacturer of personal computers. But now that Dan was no longer at the company, they had been able to tell him. It was a relief to all of them, especially since Gary and Dan had been friends for many years.

Professional considerations had not been the only reason for keeping their affair in the dark. Dan had run into troubles in the domestic and professional areas of his life at about the same time their personal lives had blossomed. Their happiness had hardly seemed the right balm for his wounds.

Maneuvering through the snowy glades and then out onto the open slope beyond, Dan realized he hadn't told them anything much about Joanna's departure, even though it had been almost nine months since she had left and he had moved north to a new job. He'd hardly had a chance. He didn't know Pauline very well, except as a work colleague, and revealing the intimacies of his private life was not really his style. At the same time, he realized he'd like a bit of time to talk to Gary. Nine months of almost complete loneliness, in a strange place and with a new company, could cause quite a freeze in the soul.

Yet he was sure that his upbeat mood today was at least partly a culmination of the past months at Triangle. He had learned so much there about real control over his working life that the effect had spilled over into the rest of his life as well. He felt effective, creative, able to tackle almost anything. At the bottom of the slope, after a little searching, he found Gary and Pauline, flushed and triumphant with their fast race downhill.

"We're going back up," said Pauline. "What would you say if we meet in the day lodge for lunch in another hour? That'll give us time for three more runs, if we're lucky."

"Fine with me," replied Dan. "In fact, I'll come with you. I think that fast run just about neutralized the last ten years for me. I've had time to think about things on the slow one, and now I'm ready to go!"

An hour and a half later, they entered the ski lodge cafeteria, where three quarters of the population of the slope was converging to devour fries and monster hamburgers.

Pauline grimaced as she took her place at the end of a line that tailed off somewhere near the door. Behind her, more people were pushing their way in, their faces flushed with the sudden change of temperature. Dan looked at the crisscross of lines ending at different counters, and realized it was no use joining her. He wanted a salad, which meant joining a different line. But then he wouldn't mind having a hamburger as well. He was ravenous.

"Pauline, can you get me a hamburger while you're there? I'll try to meet you at the checkout. Boy, this is chaotic!"

Gary had already gone to the refrigerator to get himself a cold drink. Bad move, he realized moments later. A group of very large and loudly laughing teenagers came in through the door like a tidal wave, all but drowning Pauline.

By the time Pauline had her hamburger and fries, which were rapidly growing cold, and Dan had half his lunch, Gary was still to be seen near the back of a line, swamped in the steamy breath and laughter of the crowd in front. There was no sign of an available table.

"I'm glad I'm not the manager of this restaurant," muttered Pauline under her breath. "I think I'd go commit hara-kiri off the top slope. What a mess!"

"The manager just needs a few lessons from a good manufacturing company," Dan remarked. He pointed somewhere over Pauline's head. "Quick, someone's leaving." They turned and scuttled sideways between the tightly packed tables, but they were too late. Another party, also balancing trays, got there first.

"Funny thing is," Dan went on, eyeing his rapidly cooling hamburger, "it's the same density of people on the slopes, but you don't get these bottlenecks up there: a different system of organization."

"There must be a lesson there somewhere—a table! Shoot for it!" This time they were lucky. They looked over at Gary, who made a face at them from his place in the hot food line.

As he passed a stand of potato chips, he grabbed one and held it aloft in a gesture of exaggerated triumph.

"We'd better go ahead and eat," said Pauline. "Everything's going to be cold if we don't."

"I think the lesson is simplicity," Dan said suddenly. "Going back to what you were saying earlier," he added. "The ski lift system is dead simple. One lift goes up to one area, with equal spacing between chairs and the lift moving at a constant speed. Even though people don't get on it at predictable times, it's practically impossible to get a bottleneck at the top of the slope, and there's very seldom one at the bottom either."

"I suppose people come down at a roughly equal pace," said Pauline.

"But there's a fast and a slow way down," said Gary, who had suddenly appeared with his tray.

"Yeah, but it's within predictable parameters," said Dan. "You have the conveyor belt taking the human goods to the top, then the goods distribute to one of two routes: the slow or the fast. Nothing in the system can know which way they will go. Yet, look at it. Even though there are variations in the number of people coming down, sometimes only one or two, then a group, there is never a real bottleneck. That's because the system is built to accommodate the variables."

"Meanwhile, the system delivers only what is necessary: human beings to the top of the slope," went on Gary, as he started on his moussaka, "and they have only one way to go after that: down. The laws of skiing are not much different from the laws of gravity. You know nobody is ever going to get out of line and cause a foul-up in the system because the impulse to plunge downward is stronger than anything else."

He was grinning, though whether it was at his own mild satire on Dan's theorizing or because he had finally gotten his lunch, it was hard to tell.

"That's linearity," muttered Dan. "But in here we have complexity. I've learned a lot about what that does to a process since I joined Triangle. Complexity equals chaos, at least in purchasing, manufacturing, and situations where hundreds of hungry skiers need lunch fast."

"Dan," Pauline said, looking straight at him with an exaggerated mock frown. "You're on vacation. We all are, for that matter. The whole idea of coming here was so we could forget work and chaos."

"That's hard," murmured Dan, almost as if to himself. "Going to Triangle has been a kind of revelation. It's the one good thing that came out of that mess at Rollins. Now I've experienced something so much better, it's hard not to keep thinking about it. I can hardly believe the way we were operating at that place."

"Really?" Gary looked embarrassed for a moment. "I didn't think we were that bad. We thought it was just that you and David Chan didn't hit it off."

"We didn't. But a major bone of contention was the way he blamed me for the problems in our department. He disliked me, so he traced all the foul-ups to my areas of responsibility. They landed on my desk to solve, and that's why Joanna was so furious. She couldn't believe I wasn't able to finish my job in a normal working day. You can't imagine what it was like having to solve one problem after another; situations that I had not even created in the first place."

Gary and Pauline stiffened slightly at the mention of his wife. Pauline murmured sympathetically.

"How is Joanna? I meant to ask," Gary said awkwardly. "Do you see her at all?"

"Not a look nor a word," said Dan. "She absolutely could not forgive me for those sixty-hour weeks I was putting in. She took it as a kind of unfaithfulness. I'm sure she was checking my laundry for lipstick marks. She just couldn't grasp the complexity of my work; what it was like to be supplying a large manufacturing company with parts from dozens of different vendors."

Pauline looked at Gary. "I suppose there's something to be said for working in the same department even if we do have to play ridiculous games to conceal our relationship."

"When I lost my job, that was the end. She just walked out. The mess she left was probably even worse than the mess in our department." He laughed with something like genuine merriment, he noted.

"We were constantly trying to get products out with parts that arrived late, were full of defects, or in the wrong quantities. That last fiasco—the one that got me fired—was just one in a long line. My confidence was absolutely shot by the time they 'laid me off,' as they so politely put it." An expression of self-pity, which he made no attempt to hide, appeared on his face.

"You know, I think David had it in for you," Pauline observed sympathetically. "Someone had to be the scapegoat. I don't know how anyone could have handled him any better than you. We all find him hard to work with."

"It wasn't really a case of handling David, or anyone else. It's a case of handling the system so that these foul-ups would never occur in the first place."

"Nice thought," murmured Pauline, soothingly. "But these foul-ups are part of life, aren't they? Especially life in the American corporation. We're all fallible. I doubt these things were your fault any more than anybody else's. Problem is, you were perfectly placed to be the scapegoat. Gary and I were pretty shocked at the time."

"Scapegoating seems to be a standard tool of American management," went on Dan. "I just happened to be the chosen one this time. But the fact is, there are better ways for a company to solve its problems than choosing an individual to take the blame when things go wrong. There are other methods that don't cause nearly so much pain and suffering."

Pauline was looking furtively at her new waterproof watch under the table. She glanced across at Gary with an expression of ill-concealed desperation. Gary took the cue. "Hey, Dan, don't you think we ought to get back? We've been here almost an hour. Let's talk some more tonight, okay?"

Skiing conditions were still ideal, though there were rumors that wetter snow was on the way. Dan took to the difficult slope and gave himself over to the blissful sensations of surrender to gravity, cool air whistling past his face, and the dazzling whiteness everywhere.

***

In the shared condominium, the telephone was only inches away from Dan's ear when it rang at six-thirty the next morning. Painfully, he grabbed the receiver and balanced it on his face as he rolled over onto his back. It had to be a wrong number.

"Is Gary Langden there?"

"Yeah, he is, but he's probably asleep. Can this wait?"

"Not really. This is Sam Trent from Rollins. It's rather urgent."

Dan groaned inwardly and prayed that Sam Trent, whom he knew quite well, wouldn't recognize his voice. The last thing he wanted was to get stuck in a stilted conversation about his new job and how he was doing.

"Hold on."

Gary, muttering to himself as he staggered into Dan's room, grabbed the phone and cleared his voice, trying to sound alert and efficient. "What can I do, Sam?"

"Not much from where you are. That's why I've got to ask you to get back here as soon as you can. Sorry to ruin your vacation, but that shipment from Actec has come in as rotten as a load of bad apples. The defect rate, so far, is sky-high. Somewhere around eighty percent. We're in a mess, Gary. If we don't ship those computers out to Star Systems early next week, the shortfall will be about two and a half million bucks."

Gary was holding his head, his hair flopping over his hand like the strands of black wire that he imagined crawling around the insides of several thousand low-end personal computers, which now sat forlorn in the shipping area, unable to budge.

"I don't understand it," he said. "We've never had any trouble with those chips before. The specs weren't changed. Why would a whole batch come in faulty like this?"

"Can't think," replied Sam. "Except that we were surprised they'd been delivered from Taipei instead of Singapore. We never knew anything about a change of location for manufacturing these chips."

Gary squeezed his eyes together in a gesture of exasperation. Trying to piece together the best deals on a vast array of parts had led to a situation in the purchasing department that resembled a potluck gone awry. As Pauline had once described,

"It's like having eleven desserts, a plate of cucumber salad, and a few barbecued spareribs to feed thirty people. Instead of waiting for cut-rate prices, we might be better off if we did our shopping when the parts were available, and far enough ahead of time to make sure they work."

Gary tried to speed his brain as it ran through the consequences of this calamity, but all he could feel was aching thighs. He wasn't even sure whether this mess was the result of a deal made by someone else or whether he had done it under pressure to buy cheap. He seemed to remember that he had canceled on that company once before. The one thing that stood out clearly was the impact of this delay on the quarterly figures due in three weeks. If this shipment didn't make it in time, then something else would have to compensate.

"Sorry, Sam, I'm a little hazy just now. It's early you know. Let me call you back in half an hour. I'll have something worked out."

Gary sat on the edge of Dan's bed, his head in his hands. "Looks as if the skiing is off, Dan. I'm real sorry. I'll talk to Pauline, but I think she'll agree we have to go back today. There must be some flights."

"Yeah, they go regularly from Reno; Truckee, too, I think. It's a shame to have to go back, though."

Dan went and made coffee while Gary broke the news to Pauline. Sitting in the breakfast nook, they tried to come up with a strategy.

"Didn't Actec tell you these chips would be coming from their other plant?" Pauline asked.

"I suppose they did," Gary replied, looking defensive. He was finding it hard now to ignore memories of putting this company under heavy pressure to produce and then calling the deal off under pressures of his own. Was it surprising if they didn't go out of their way to keep him informed? "But that was no call for action. After all, they've been manufacturing in both places for as long as we've been doing business with them. A chip from one location is as good as another, as long as the specs remain the same."

"Not the case," cautioned Pauline, a look of regret on her

face. "Batches, even from one location, can differ quite a lot. I bought a dozen skeins of blue wool for a needlepoint pillow I was doing once. Went back to get two more, when I ran out, and the color was different by the tiniest shade. I couldn't use it at all. Took months before I could find matching yarn to finish that pillow cover."

The phone rang again, sounding demanding and worrisome in light of the events of the morning. It was Mary Garr, a friend of Pauline's and a previous roommate.

"I hate to bother you, but your company's been on the phone. A guy named Sam Trent called and said they've got some problem. I didn't tell him where you were, obviously, but I said I'd call you. I hate to do this to you. How's the skiing?"

"Thanks, Mary. I already got the message. The skiing was great. They'd already called Gary." She soon concluded the call, and turned to Dan. "I had to leave my old roommate's phone number with the company so they wouldn't know about Gary and me. It's so ridiculous to have to play these games. No dating other employees allowed, you know—much less more serious relationships."

They breakfasted in a hurry, Gary gesticulating with his toast as he talked to the local airport. "Seems there's no flight to Orange County till eleven-fifteen," he said as he put the phone down. "Gorgeous day," Pauline said regretfully, looking out the window at the crystalline light flashing off the new fall of snow.

***

As they sat in the tiny Truckee airport lounge, the consequences of the mess back at Rollins started to spell themselves out.

"You know, the quarter ends on February 28," observed Gary. "If this shipment doesn't show up in the sales figures, the company's going to make a disastrous showing."

"We're making good progress on the orders for Congden and that big computer retailer; is it Byte World?" said Pauline. "We may be able to deliver those early if we work like hell, and save the figures."

Gary looked doubtful. "They may not want early ship-
ments," he said. "It's a case of screwing up their warehouse
space. They won't have budgeted in such a big shipment either.
Byte World didn't ask for delivery till April."

"We'll just have to negotiate, and then work our asses off."
Pauline gave him a look that was quite unlike the ones Dan had
seen passing between her and Gary for the past two days. She
looked furious.

"You mean take a discount," said Dan, feeling this might be
the moment to intervene. To him, such discussions were only
too familiar. Listening to them, he realized with surprise how
few crises of this sort he had experienced during the past nine
months he had been at Triangle. Already, his mind was working
differently. He was getting used to a calmer climate, where he
could think about changing situations for the better: improving
processes, and preventing snarl-ups, instead of spending all his
time troubleshooting problems.

"Just hearing you guys is giving me goose bumps," he said.
"It's bringing all that misery back: constant headaches of one
kind or another. How do you stand it?"

Gary and Pauline were both staring at him. They were
dumbfounded, never having imagined that life as a buyer could
be any different from their experiences. They couldn't relate to
his attitude. "So all your headaches are in the past, now that
you're at terrific Triangle?" Pauline inquired with a sarcastic
edge to her voice.

"Well, you know I hadn't even been aware of it, but I think
the worst of them may be," said Dan. "I'm working a perfectly
normal week, home by five-thirty or so every day. At first I used
to feel guilty about getting off so early, but everyone else was
doing it too, and we were leaving a department that we didn't
mind coming back to every morning. Ironic really," he added in
an undertone, "with Joanna gone."

"So what's the secret, Dan?" asked Gary gloomily, his expression of preoccupied cynicism belying the question. "Well,
as a matter of fact, I've been trying to tell you. You weren't too
keen to hear about my enthusiasm for our methods though. I
understand. We did come here to ski, after all."

"Try us again," said Pauline. "There's not much else to do now."

"Well, for one thing, we communicate with our suppliers a tremendous amount, whether deliveries are expected or not. It's like a constant monitoring, almost as if they're part of our company. And we don't play dirty tricks on them, like making rush orders and then canceling at the last minute."

"Sounds impossible," said Gary, remembering times when he had done just that: fairly recently, in fact, and with the same company that had sent in the dud batch of parts. "Do you ever get off the phone? I can't imagine talking to people in four dozen companies every day. A lot of our vendors are thousands of miles away too. How big did you say Triangle was?"

"About two hundred million dollars a year. Four hundred employees."

"Wow. So how many vendors?"

"For the high-end electronics goods I deal with, twelve."

"How do you manage with so few?" asked Pauline. "I mean, it sounds almost impossible. You can't have any backup for parts with that few."

"We don't," replied Dan. "But we don't need backup because each of the suppliers we work with is a hundred percent reliable."

"Sounds like Disneyland," said Gary. "Everything clean and everyone smiling all day. Why is it that all our vendors are unreliable while all yours are reliable? What's so special about Rollins that we make such bad choices?"

"It's not the company or the suppliers themselves," replied Dan. "It's the way they work together."

Gary looked at his watch. "You'd better tell us quick," he said. "It's ten-fifty. We're going to have to board our plane soon."

"Well, it's the difference between your wife and the girl you're dating, I suppose," Dan said slowly. "We know our suppliers like we know ourselves. We know their plants and their methods. In fact, Triangle taught them most of it. My manufacturing manager, John, is always beating the drum for consistent methodology. He's a born teacher. Never lets a day go past without drumming home lessons about reducing complexity and increasing linearity."

"You mean he uses Just-in-Time, statistical quality control, techniques like that?" put in Gary. "That's all good stuff, especially in manufacturing. But we couldn't do much with it."

"Sure you could," Dan contradicted. "I see it done every day. In fact, that stuff works much better if you extend it right through the system. It certainly doesn't stop with manufacturing. The suppliers use the same techniques we do. And it's not just talk. It's action. John puts into practice everything he preaches. I've seen him clean up a department with a few swift strokes: diagnosis, decision, and the glitches are on their way out."

Gary and Pauline were still incredulous at what they were hearing. "So what happens if your carefully cultivated vendor's plant burns down in the night?" asked Pauline. "Your bridges are burned too, aren't they? Who takes over the job then?"

"That's a good question," conceded Dan. "And you're not the first one to ask it." He paused, thinking. "Assuming it's only the plant that burns, we still have the brains of everyone on both sites, and their intimate knowledge of one another's situations. There's a real powerhouse available if you have two companies working in tandem."

"Such a perfect marriage that property means nothing?" said Pauline, her eyes narrow. "And how do you arrange such an ideal partnership?"

"Well, I suppose it's the same deal," replied Dan. "You share your dreams. In our case, that means sharing our data bases. You've got to provide communication constantly, like Billy Joel says."

"What do you mean? You give them your Material Requirements Planning?" asked Gary in surprise.

"Absolutely. That's what I've been saying. It makes for very direct and simple communication. If a supervisor from the supplier company is working closely with one of our purchasing managers, he can tune into our MRP and have a clear idea from day to day what our requirements will be. Of course, that wouldn't work if we had several suppliers for the same product. Such honesty only works in a monogamous relationship."

Gary and Pauline looked at each other. Their faces, which had been strained, softened for a moment into laughter. Dan chalked up a score—on the personal level, if not as a consultant.

"I never imagined purchasing could be so romantic," said Pauline.

"We send love letters too," Dan went on, warming to his theme. "Electronic mail over our computers. The systems are linked. It's lots of fun!"

The flight to Orange County was called over the squeaky loudspeaker. Gary and Pauline got up and Dan followed.

"I hope we'll be able to continue these exciting sessions of marital therapy for companies and their vendors," Gary said. Dan couldn't tell whether he was joking or really meant it. "Pauline and I might even learn something on a personal level."

"We may need to, the way I feel now," said Pauline as she kissed Dan on the cheek. "Sorry to leave you like this. We'll call. I'd like to try and get back up here later in the week, but it depends how bad the mess is down there." She looked hard at Gary, indicating that he wouldn't be allowed to get off lightly for this crime against their vacation.

Dan turned and walked through the swinging door. Although he was alone again, he felt surprisingly good. The intensity of learning over the past few months had prevented him from sitting down and reflecting on the merits of his new job. Though he had begun to appreciate it on the slope yesterday morning, it took telling someone else to make him realize just how impressed, even excited, he was. He found himself smiling as he opened the door to his car. He felt like someone in the know; someone with something to offer. There was no doubt about it. Triangle was one heck of a company!

***

Sitting with his legs stretched out in front of the television on Tuesday evening, Dan was interrupted by the telephone. It was Gary.

"Dan, we're hoping to get back up there again, maybe on Thursday morning. We've paid for the condo after all. I'm damned if we're going to waste our whole vacation! How's the snow?"

"Near perfect. We never got that wet spell they were talking about, though we could have done with a bit more dry snow. But I can't complain. How's it going down there?"

"We're beginning to see our way through the mess. It's been a hell of a thirty-six hours though. Pauline is furious with me. There's no longer a problem trying to conceal our relationship. Anyone would rate us arch enemies to look at her face. When your work goes to hell, your home life does too. I see what you went through now and I keep thinking there's got to be an easier way."

"There is. I just wish it hadn't taken me so long to find it." Dan realized he was in danger of sounding evangelical; enough to put anyone off wanting to know more about his company. But to his surprise, Gary didn't try to sidestep the subject.

"You know, I wasn't in the mood to hear about it before, but I think I'd like to find out what's going on up there in that company in rainy Oregon. The way I feel just now, I might even come and join you, if it's really as good as it sounds."

Dan groaned aloud. "Come and grab my promotion opportunity, like you did at Rollins. Is that what you have in mind?" he said jokingly. Gary was a little older than Dan and had always held a job senior to his.

"Okay, okay, I'll compromise," said Gary. "I'll just sit and listen to you in Tahoe. In light of what's been going on down here, some of what you said is beginning to make real sense."

Dan tried not to let his grin come across on the phone. "Shall I come and pick you up at the airport?"

"No, no. Keep skiing. You've got to do enough to make up for our lost days. We'll find our own way over. See you on Thursday evening, assuming nothing else goes wrong."

***

It was a contemplative evening. As they sat around the fondue dish, chasing the warm, wine-saturated Gruyère with pronged chunks of bread, Dan tried to pry the lowdown out of Gary as tactfully as possible. "So, did you solve the problem?" he asked.

"Not really; not from my point of view anyway. The part was technically within spec, so they wouldn't admit any mistake, and won't take the stuff back. This was an expedited order, so they were under pressure. They didn't tell me they didn't have the capacity in their Singapore plant. They manufactured in Taipei, and everything came out a little different. But that one little variation made all the difference between a functioning computer and a dead one."

"You know, we've pushed that company around an awful lot lately," said Pauline. Her "we" was clearly meant to refer to Gary. "They've had a number of rush orders, and a few that we canceled at the last minute. They're getting tough with us now; refusing to take stuff back, and demanding overtime expenses due to the expedited order."

"I'll have to take the blame," said Gary miserably, staring at the pale green meniscus glowing in his wine glass. "It'll appear on the purchase price variance, no doubt." Dan looked sympathetic. "I've been starting to realize that it's the material flow that's killing a lot of companies," said Dan. "Managers talk all the time about people: labor, motivation, how they can improve output. Productivity is traditionally measured by output per person per hour worked. So the people get blamed. What they don't look at is the way the system is screwing up the best of human efforts."

"You can say that again," said Pauline, taking an appreciative sip of chardonnay. "From the way things were when we got back on Monday, it looks as if Gary might be the next one to walk the plank."

"I'm not surprised," said Dan. "Looking back at Rollins after nine months at Triangle, I feel as if I'm watching the proverbial emperor fiddle while Rome burns. I used to think it was inevitable. But now I can see that the constant snarl-ups, crises piling one on top of the other, are really unnecessary. Inexcusable, in fact. Sorry. I hope that doesn't sound critical of you guys. I'm just learning the alternatives myself, so I have no right to be smug."

"Okay," muttered Gary through fondue. "There's no question we could be doing a lot better."

"D'you realize how much better?" asked Dan emphatically. "If IC houses shipped linearly, they could make two or three times what most of them make now."

"Are you kidding us?" Pauline said. "What have you been smoking, Dan? They don't receive orders linearly. And that's our problem, too. We don't know from one minute to the next what we're going to have to produce."

"Buying is more complicated than manufacturing, in a lot of ways," observed Gary. "It depends so heavily on forecasting. And the forecasts are often right out of whack. We have to make last-minute adjustments, which sometimes turn out to be right on—and sometimes right off."

"The system is insensitive to change," said Dan. "Yet change is what we're dealing with, every day. It's the element we live in. With all these variables, the buyers are supposed to end up with exactly the right amount of material for the job as it stands when it goes through manufacturing."

"Not too soon or too late either," added Pauline.

"That's why, if you don't mind my saying so again, you've got to keep your finger on the pulse and let your suppliers keep their fingers on it, too. Our suppliers are so much a part of Triangle that they get paid by how many completed units we ship. We don't pay them for parts per piece. It avoids a lot of paperwork, and cuts down the cost of the finished unit."

"I still don't see how that can prevent a lot of the events that throw our calculations off."

"Well, you must admit, better communication with Actec wouldn't have been a bad thing," Pauline said, giving Gary a sidelong look that indicated he was lucky to be forgiven (by her, at least).

"All right, all right," he said, "you pronounced your verdict on me before anyone else in the court. But I've taken my punishment. Stop beating me, please!"

"But cutting down on suppliers is not only better for communications," Dan said, appearing not to have noticed this exchange. "It also cuts costs by a large margin. The time saved in negotiating and communicating with one supplier instead of several different ones really does free up a lot of manpower to do other things. I've actually had time to set up measurements to find out how accurate our forecasting is. I would never have managed an enterprise like that at Rollins."

"So, okay, it's good for management time. But you said yourself that labor isn't really the issue."

"Right. There's a lot more to it than that. With one supplier of any given part, we don't have to inspect so often. You see, they have taken on board our philosophy of statistical measurement of their processes. We keep paring down our complexity, in tandem, and comparing notes about results. Many of the suppliers are so reliable now that we've been able to cut out the quality inspector's job altogether."

"*Our* philosophy, is it?" repeated Pauline, archly raising her eyebrows. "You really are a born-again quality fiend."

"Not really," replied Dan evenly. "I'm just a lazy jerk who's happy his life is so much easier. Seeing what sort of a dismal state you are in, I think you two could take a dose of the same medicine. Why suffer when you don't have to?"

"Right, that was another point about labor," said Gary, putting down his fondue fork and counting on his fingers. "Now give us some hard evidence about improving the system: material flow and so on."

"Okay. Defects from one of our key suppliers went down from nineteen percent this time last year to seven-tenths of a percent as of this month. I was looking over the statistics that have already been compiled on this while setting up some of my own. Our own defect rate on the computer that uses that part has dropped to one percent, though we're still intending to do better. So are the suppliers. You can't quarrel with that."

"Perfectionists all," remarked Gary, offhandedly.

"Of course," replied Dan, beginning to sound defensive. "There's no point of diminishing returns. That's one little axiom that gets thrown around in the company. Our manufacturing manager is big on Deming. One of his first points is, *Improve constantly and forever.*"

He paused. "You two behave as if I'm making all this up.

Why are you so cynical? I've never seen anyone need help so badly."

Pauline laughed. "I suppose we have to sound skeptical to stop ourselves from drooling. You can't imagine how we'd love Rollins to be achieving results like that."

"Oh, and by the way," Dan held his hand up with mock authority, "due to the reduction in oversupply of parts, backups, shortages, defects, floor space, scrap, and rework . . ."

". . . all bogeys zapped at once, of course!"

". . . the price per unit goes down, and that saving is passed on to the customer. Now that is a portrait of a competitive American company, don't you think?"

"It sounds okay," said Gary. "But you still haven't really told us how all this can help the purchasers. I need personal help at the moment, don't you see. I'm in a damn bad place!"

Dan got up and rummaged among the smoldering logs with the poker. "This needs stoking up a bit," he said, ignoring the question. "Oh yes, and I forgot to tell you, by going to one supplier, you avoid all that expensive tooling several times over for specialized parts. That can really help reduce the product's price."

He blew on the fire, and a small flame started to dance. "We really need a bellows for this. Uncivilized place."

Gary and Pauline exchanged glances. "Yes," said Pauline, drawing out the syllable. "We're waiting."

"Okay," Dan sat on the floor with a thud. "Well, one thing I remember about Rollins was that the purchasers were always second-guessing the forecast. We'd change schedules at the last moment, decrease inventories, and override forecasts when they turned out to be inaccurate. That led to a lot of panic orders, then withdrawing of orders, causing all kinds of chaos. . . ."

"Shortages and backups all over the place," Pauline added.

"At Triangle, we do fairly short-term forecasts, based on a lot of factors. We keep our ears to the ground, keep a close eye on markets and currencies, and are always open to change; until we freeze the forecast."

"Frozen forecast," said Pauline contemplatively. "Shall we have it for dessert? We don't seem to have anything else."

"So, total openness followed by total rigidity," remarked Gary.

"In a way," went on Dan. "It sounds rigid, but until frozen, the system is very responsive to change. You see, at some point, all the cooks have to be using the same recipe. Otherwise, everything ends up a mess. You risk losing your suppliers and your customers."

"But how can you know the forecast is accurate at the point you freeze it?" asked Gary, pouring out more chardonnay.

"We can't be certain, and nothing is perfect. You have to be realistic about some degree of inaccuracy. There are too many factors. Some of them—like market forces, currencies, and price changes for materials—are simply too unpredictable to allow us to achieve complete accuracy. But even if some aspects of it are wrong, things usually even themselves out; or that's the common wisdom at Triangle. We do use SQC to look at the accuracy of the forecast, so we're trying to find out what factors lead to the worst inaccuracies."

"Well, if you can't guarantee the accuracy by freezing forecasts, I'm not sure I can see the point," Pauline said as she curled herself into the corner of the couch.

"Well, at least it is predictable once it's frozen," said Dan. "You don't screw up your suppliers and your purchasing department with orders that keep changing. That way, you keep your relationships with your best suppliers. They can trust you to take what you order, after a certain point in the month. In exchange, they don't drop you in order to accommodate a customer who offers to pay them more. It builds stability, and loyalty, but there's still room for most of the variables."

Gary shifted on the couch, and started to rub one of his ankles. But his expression was preoccupied. "It sounds as if there might be something there. But of course, theories always sound so good. It's when you try putting them into practice that they fall apart at the seams."

"Well, I suppose it's a case of learning how to use them," said Dan. "It's like a piano. It may be the best piano made, but you can't expect it to sound sensational unless you put some time and effort into learning to play."

"So you've learned to play the great piano of quality at Triangle, have you?"

"I'm a novice. I'm learning. But even now it's working for me—mainly because so many other people around me do it well. I keep picking things up from them. It's more like breathing a stronger concentration of oxygen than being taught. I just feel better. Things go better. Maybe it's more like playing in an orchestra than playing the piano. When I make a squeak on my bassoon, the strings cover up the sound. Even when I have to make a bit of effort, setting up Pareto charts, for example, I like it!" He grinned.

Pauline and Gary were both suddenly smiling at him. "You know, I just realized," said Gary, "you look happier than I've seen you for years. Maybe you have got something going up there. It sounds like such a mix of theories though. I have to admit, I find your description confusing."

"Well, it's probably hard to describe because it's gone well beyond the theoretical stage. It really comes from the top guy, and the people who work with him. It's a way of life; not much is written down. You just catch it when you come into the company—like a benign virus."

Pauline laughed. Looking at her watch she said, "You know, it's late. We ought to go to bed if we're going to get onto the slopes in good time tomorrow." She pushed the logs to the back of the grate with a poker. "Fire's almost out anyway," she observed, yawning. "I think it's telling us something."

As they got up, stretching, Gary asked: "Any chance I could get a tour of this facility of yours?"

Dan's smile grew wide. "No problem," he said. "I'll call you early next week."

***

Next morning, Gary and Pauline did not appear at their usual early hour. When Gary finally shuffled into the kitchen to put on the kettle, Dan was fully dressed and ready to hit the slopes.

"What hit you, Gary? You look bombed out."

"I'm bushed. We've been talking all night."

Dan laughed. "I'm serious," Gary went on. "That conversation we had last night really got us going. I don't think we're up to skiing. All I want to do is sit in the hot-tub and steam my brain."

"I never knew this had affected you so much."

"Hey, I've just realized I can't go on living like this. I'll be a lonely old man who mutters to himself before I know it, if this kind of scenario keeps repeating itself."

Pauline walked into the kitchen, pulling her robe around her. "I think we've got a revolution on our hands, Dan. You see the two founders of it here in this kitchen. Later when they write the history books, you'll say 'I was there at the moment when they saw the light.'"

"Buyers unite to bring sanity back into their lives!" said Gary, waving his mug. Dan sat down. It was clear he wouldn't be getting out onto the slopes early.

"You know, Dan, we realized that buyers are key people in this crazy game of business," said Pauline, pouring coffee. "But we're at the mercy of so many factors. Ruthless competition, executives who want growth at any cost. We've been resorting to every trick in the book, just to conform to these crazy schedules. It's like being on a runaway roller coaster in someone else's nightmare."

"We make a lot of the deals ourselves, but half our problems come from trying to fulfill someone else's blueprint for this month's productivity figures. Dreams are put together on paper for the benefit of the shareholders and then we're expected to make them come true. Meantime, we screw up everyone: our suppliers, the people on the production line who have to work overtime to make up for late materials . . ."

". . . and ourselves, most of all," put in Pauline. "I realized last night that I've been thinking like all the other bad guys: Blaming individuals for faults that are built into the system." She went over to Gary and ruffled his hair. "This individual in particular," she said fondly.

"Well, Gary's lucky that you understand," said Dan. "I guess you need to see it firsthand to believe it. At least you know what he's talking about."

"We're going to make some pretty resounding changes when we get back. But we'll need your help," said Gary. Dan looked at the pair of them, sitting huddled together with tousled hair like babes in the wood, and couldn't help laughing. This image contrasted so strongly with the one they usually cultivated—and normally deserved—of two highly competent and assured senior buyers.

Instinctively, he held out his hands to them. "I'll do my best. But, remember, I'm still learning too. Welcome to the adventure."

***

LESSONS FROM THE BUYER'S STORY

Which Kind of System: Complex or Linear?

The chapter begins with concrete illustrations of two very different kinds of systems, represented by the restaurant and the ski slope. In the restaurant, people and materials (food) flow unevenly and awkwardly through the line, causing delays (people waiting in lines and for tables) and poor quality (cold food).

By contrast, the ski slope shows how things can run smoothly when there is a known bottleneck (in this case, the ski lift) which restricts the flow of people through the system. Variation (the random way in which people choose the fast or slow runs) has less effect on the system than the random choice of food which people make in the restaurant.

Though Pauline is distressed at the condition of the restaurant, she takes for granted a situation which is just as chaotic: the one at Rollins. For her, complexity is the norm, a fact of life. Crises, both actual and concocted, are the rule. The traditional attitude of management is that if there are no crises, people are not working hard enough.

As the situation at Rollins gets worse, the buyers make frantic, reactive adjustments to the changing conditions, with little understanding of what is actually going on. In the technical terms of SQC, this is called tampering, or making changes without understanding the system's behavior. The buyers would probably be better off doing nothing, because tampering makes things worse.

Deming and others use a practical demonstration to illustrate tampering. In the demonstration, a small marble is dropped fifty times through a funnel onto a table in an attempt to hit a marked target. Results are plotted on a chart to establish how close each drop gets to the target, and thus identify the random behavior of the system. Then, during three additional rounds of dropping the marble, different sets of rules for moving the funnel are employed to show how variation and error are compounded by any misguided attempts to adjust for accuracy. Moving the funnel in any manner yields worse results.

The system at Rollins does not accommodate change, as Dan observes. Worse yet, Rollins' own quarterly sales goals are creating even more complexity because they are forcing everyone, including the buyers, to sacrifice the company's long-term interests in order to make the numbers look good on the short-term reports.

For Discussion:

✓ What specifically did the Rollins buyers do to "move the funnel"?

✓ Why must you understand your system before trying to change it?

Scapegoating Changes Nothing

As Dan has come to understand after he has left Rollins, scapegoating, or blaming those who have no control over a situation, does not bring the situation under control. People's professional and personal lives are not lived in isolation, as Dan's failed marriage and Gary's and Pauline's relationship demonstrate, and scapegoating only further impairs people's ability to do their jobs. Scapegoating inevitably leads to fractionalization, as everyone reacts defensively to the risk of being blamed.

When Gary becomes the victim of the scapegoating at Rollins, it threatens to harm his relationship with Pauline. His pain and desperation finally cause him to examine his old assumptions, listen to Dan, and change his views of what a purchasing system should be. Once he and Pauline have changed, there are several things they can do. They can work within Rollins to change the system as they intend to at the end of the story, or they can associate themselves with an employer such as Triangle, whose philosophy is more compatible with their new understanding.

For Discussion:
- ✓ What are the assumptions behind scapegoating?
- ✓ Why is scapegoating irrelevant at a company such as Triangle?

Making Forecasts Work for the Company

Dan explains to Gary and Pauline how Triangle's forecasting system combines the best of flexibility and rigidity. Flexibility throughout part of the month allows for adjustments to the inevitable changes. But, when the forecast is frozen, everyone, including Triangle's suppliers, can be confident that all the others will go with it. They can put their efforts toward quality work without the fear that eleventh-hour changes will be made.

By continually refining the system, Triangle can obtain reasonable accuracy from the forecast. More important, negative factors such as frantic deal-making, rush orders, and last-minute cancellations can be avoided. Over the long run, product quality can improve, and products can be delivered on time.

For Discussion:
- ✓ How does this combination of flexible and rigid forecasting help groups within a company cooperate?
- ✓ In what other activities or departments could this way of doing things be useful?

No More Deals: Building Trust with Suppliers

Both manufacturing and purchasing at Rollins have degenerated into chaos, and people have lost sight of the benefits of uniform production. People are trying to control the system by making deals: negotiating with customers to accept "bad" or inaccurate orders; and with vendors to supply parts on unrealistic schedules or at unrealistic prices.

To make things worse, purchasing often cancels "rush" orders, or asks vendors to take back parts, because Rollins' needs change incessantly. In trying to end up with the best deals, the purchasing department instead has many angry vendors of varying reliability. Dan explains to Gary and Pauline that they need to think of vendors as suppliers who are extensions of Rollins' own production capability. Unlike vendors, with whom we have brief, superficial interaction, suppliers have an ongoing relationship with a company and help the organization sell to the end user.

By establishing aboveboard, ongoing relationships with a select group of suppliers, purchasing can reduce complexity. The true value of each supplier is the talent and dedication of its people, not the parts it supplies. As Gary learns from the fiasco with the bad chips, specifications and drawings do not always control product quality.

By working together, Rollins and its suppliers could develop backup plans for emergencies, so that the crises that constantly threaten Gary's and Pauline's careers can be avoided. Rollins needs to start building trust with long-term suppliers, so that there can be open communication and free exchange of information. Through daily communication, Rollins and its suppliers would then keep up with the quickly changing forecasts and be able to work cooperatively, instead of being adversaries.

With fewer suppliers, and with all parties constantly trying to reduce the complexity between them, each one will have more time to improve its own system. Achieving linearity in manufacturing is a great, valuable accomplishment. Dan shows Pauline and Gary that purchasing and other "soft" quality areas have a vital role to play, and that, by improving their own department's processes with statistical quality control, Just-in-Time, and other techniques, the entire company will begin to improve and prosper.

For Discussion:

✓ Why was Rollins' emphasis on negotiating on price with vendors so damaging?

✓ How can computers be used to help suppliers and customers communicate?

3

THE ENGINEER'S STORY
One Step Back, Two Steps Forward

"TREVOR LEONIS ON the phone, Jim. Line five."

Jim Bernstein smiled as he reached for his phone. There was never a call from Trevor that didn't somehow change the course of his day.

"Good to hear you, Trevor. How goes it?"

"Jim, can you have lunch with me today?"

Jim glanced at his watch. It was just past ten o'clock. He was planning to meet with the supervisors in his department at lunch time. But there was no contradicting Trevor Leonis, his friend and mentor for many years. Besides, since Trevor's company had been taken over and he'd been promoted, they had seen very little of each other.

"What could possibly be this urgent?" Jim asked jokingly. "You've ignored me for the past two months."

"You'll find out. What time would suit you?"

Jim did some quick mental calculations. "Make it late? Say, one o'clock."

"Fine. I thought we'd go to the Skipper, just across the street from you. I'll meet you in your office first."

When Trevor's large form appeared in the doorway at 12:59, Jim found himself perspiring with nervous anticipation, though he wasn't sure why.

"Sorry not to give you more warning, Jim," Trevor said in his customary growl.

"I'm happy you called. It's been a long time since we've had a chance to talk. How are things in your territory?"

"Well, I've had some interesting problems on my hands since Unitis was taken over." Their feet dented the plush green of the newly landscaped lawns as they walked. "It turns out that Yarrow's manufacturing is in a far worse mess than we ever suspected."

Jim looked at him in surprise. Yarrow, Inc., was a highly reputable giant in the computer world. Their YR2 personal computer had dominated the market for the past two and a half years. "Their figures look good," he replied, pushing open the heavy wooden door of the restaurant.

"Of course. But you know how misleading figures can be. Their inventory problems are horrendous. The YR2 is not selling, frankly because it's passé. They should be bringing out the next generation."

"So why aren't they? They have an enormous product development lab. They've got some great people in there, too, from what I hear."

Trevor bared his teeth in a smile that led people to nickname him "the Saint Bernard," not because of his goodness, but because of his resemblance to that massive and hairy dog. "That's precisely what I want to talk to you about. I'm hoping you might be able to help." His jowls shook slightly as he looked directly at Jim.

Jim looked puzzled. "You mean on the inventory problem?" A furrow appeared between his eyes.

"Not so much on the inventory, though that needs to be dealt with, too. No, I want to ask you to come and work with me. My plan is that you should take over the Yarrow lab and straighten out their development processes."

Jim stared at him, amazed that he would make such a preposterous proposal. He wondered if Trevor had gone crazy under the stress of the merger.

"Trevor, I'm not an engineer. I don't see how I could possibly help. I'd be in no position to tell them anything they don't already know about development processes."

"I think you would, as a matter of fact. We need to try to

do something different." Trevor nodded as the waiter handed them oversize menus. "Why don't we order, and then I'll explain. The Hawaiian ahi is good."

They paused to order. Then Trevor shifted on his small chair and leaned forward. "Okay, Jim, as I was saying, we need to do something different, and we need your help. This is the way I see it. Yarrow is not getting product out. They were manufacturing like mad, but they're not selling. Frankly, that YR2 computer has had its day, and they know it. More advanced computers are on the market and the YR2 is only holding its own because it looks like a safe option."

Jim's face was frozen. What made Trevor think that he, vice president of operations in a highly successful small company that gave him a great deal of credit for its success, would want to give up all that to take over a gigantic mess like the one he was describing?

"Trevor, I don't understand. My expertise is in manufacturing. That's the only thing I know. You need someone like Vic Walton. He's a brilliant product designer, and he's not too happy where he is at the moment."

Salads appeared on the table. Trevor tackled his with relish. "No, Jim. You're not understanding me. He's not the guy I need. The problem, as far as I understand it, is this. The lab is suffocating because there's just too much complexity. When I talk to the product development people, they think things are normal and that we just need more people."

"What they need is not more people but a new point of view," Jim broke in.

Trevor looked as pleased as a dog that's just caught a ball smack in its mouth. "I *knew* you'd understand this problem, Jim, so don't pretend you don't! You're right. It's not a lack of people, or even of promising products. We have plenty of both. The trouble is, the completion of each product is taking far too long, and nobody can get at the reasons why. One thing I am sure of: We don't need to throw resources at them. Just the opposite, in fact. We need someone who'll reduce complexity."

Jim nodded thoughtfully. "I still don't understand how their figures look so good if they're selling as badly as you say."

"They take their costs against the unit when they sell, not against current profits."

"Well, they say you can accrue anything," commented Jim.

"Right. That computer sold well for a long time, and they haven't yet adjusted to the fact that it's not selling any more. They're fooling themselves into thinking this is just a market turndown and we'll have a surge of demand. Past demand has been so high that it's almost a reflex response with that division to think they should build up inventory. But it's clear to me that the whole manufacturing division is now in a holding pattern. It's making YR2s for lack of anything better to do."

"So we're back to the problems in the development lab. New products are being held up for some reason. What's the reason?" Jim said.

"You tell me," Trevor replied, eyeing Jim meaningfully.

"You're seriously asking me to tackle this, Trevor? Product development has never been my field."

"They need to get control of their processes."

"Look, Trevor, the engineers will never stand for it. Can you imagine them submitting themselves to the scrutiny of a manufacturing expert, like a bunch of kindergarten kids having their hands inspected?"

"I know, I know." Trevor's hand swooped down upon his ice water and he took an enthusiastic swig. "But we can be more subtle about it than that. We don't have to tread on their precious creativity."

"I'm not sure how you'd conceal what you're doing. Engineers take a fierce pride in their work. They want to be recognized when they come out with a product that's never been done before. You can't make their work look as if it's the product of a system rather than a group of people. They'll be walking out in droves."

Trevor sighed. "Jim," he said slowly, "if you work with me, I think we could move our understanding of process control a major step forward. This is unexplored territory. It's risky, of course, but it could be the next big discovery. I'm offering you a job at a ten billion dollar company. If this works, it'll work big."

Jim took a long draught of water and pushed away his plate. "Trevor," he said apologetically, "I don't think I'm your man. I appreciate your confidence in me, but I'm not good at upheavals, and I'm not an engineer. That's a big department where people have been doing things in their own way for a long time. I think you need someone whom they'll accept more readily; someone with an engineering background."

Trevor looked thoughtful. He stared hard at a print of an iridescent, oversize trout that hung just above the level of their heads. "D'you happen to remember a conversation we had about eight years ago? I think, at the Fingus Restaurant?"

"We were eating fish then, too, I remember. You introduced me to abalone." Jim smiled, a rueful expression appearing on his face.

"I introduced you to more than abalone. That was the conversation that decided us to go ahead with a different program at Galloway Electronics. Remember?" Trevor's blue eyes were fixed on him with a mischievous glare.

"Trevor, you're not playing fair," Jim said. "I won't be pressured like this."

"And what happened?" Trevor went on, pretending he hadn't heard. "We took a booster rocket to that company and pushed it from forty million dollars to five hundred million dollars in a couple of years."

"*You* did it, Trevor. I just watched . . . and helped a bit."

"*We* did it together. You're the best manufacturing person I know, Jim. I wouldn't be beating you up like this if I didn't believe it." He gave him a beatific smile and hailed the waiter for the check.

***

On the second day of Jim's employment at Yarrow, Inc., Brad Ortez, deputy lab manager, was waiting for him, wearing a look as inviting as a concrete wall. They had been over problems the day before, and Jim had spent much of the night pondering what he'd learned.

"We obviously have to reduce cycle times," Jim was saying.

"I'd like to use some of the same process control ideas that we use in manufacturing."

Brad looked as if he'd smelled leaking gas. "Process control? In product development? How would that apply?"

"I think it would apply plenty. This isn't orthodox, I know, but I think we could reduce waste the same way we do in manufacturing. We just have to think of communication and organizational processes in a material kind of way."

"But we're talking about repetitive situations in manufacturing," Brad objected. He was breathing faster and his face was a shade ruddier. "We can't take statistical measurements of our product engineers' thought processes."

"Maybe not their thought processes," said Jim. He could feel himself faltering under the glare of Brad's disdain. "But we can measure other things, like the areas where time is unaccounted for: all meetings, information gathering, communication between engineers and support staff."

"If we have people collecting data and punching time clocks, they'll leave," Brad said bluntly. "They're already working twelve hours a day, sometimes seven days a week. If you start micromanaging them, they'll walk out—and I'll be the first person to go."

Jim realized this would be a pitched battle. At least the hostility was out in the open where he could deal with it. "Brad, the YR3 is the priority. Everyone agrees on that."

"Yeah, everyone's working on it, too."

Jim took aim and hurled his first spear. "I've already been around the lab this morning, and asked everyone what they were working on. Nobody was working on the YR3."

Brad blinked and recovered. He did not want anyone to see he'd been hit in the eye. "Well, we're waiting for the CAD-CAM to design the boards. We're also waiting for marketing to get back to us with more design specs."

For a moment, Jim felt a strange sense of relief. There was a familiar ring to this story. He'd met its equivalent in manufacturing many times. He said, "You mean we're already building the prototype and the information for the design isn't complete?"

Brad looked at him defensively. "We always have to change the design. Marketing refines the specifications as they learn more about what the customer wants."

"So as far as I can tell, nobody is working on the YR3. Everyone is waiting for something."

"We're supposed to have a meeting this afternoon with marketing. They'll give us some idea of their plans then."

"Are these the final details you need before you can go ahead?" Jim asked. He knew the answer before it came.

"No, there'll be more."

"D'you know what they are?" asked Jim. He had his opponent backed up against a wall.

Jim reminded himself, Brad's not the enemy, the complexity is. He was feeling an unreasonable charge of energy as he ran clues to ground. It was important not to let it look like personal aggression or blame.

Brad almost visibly leaned away from him. "Not yet. But they'll probably result in some redesign."

Jim scratched his head and looked puzzled. "So, Brad, what are people doing?"

"Oh, we have lots of other projects we're working on. A range of modems and a server, for example."

"D'you have all the information for those?" Jim asked. He wished Brad would come up with one good blow on his own behalf, if only to save face.

"No," he answered. "Some are out for review. We're waiting for them; they'll probably be in next week." He waved his arms vaguely.

Jim paused and gazed hard at the tan carpeted floor. "Brad, tell me this. If you had all the information right now for the YR3, how long would it take you to get it ready for manufacturing? That is, assuming nobody objected to the design."

Brad calculated a moment. "Oh, we could have it ready for production—easily in two months."

For the first time, they looked at one another. A kind of realization dawned on Brad's broad face.

"Then why are we scheduling it for production four or five quarters out?" Jim asked.

"We've planned three iterations of design to make sure it meets everything marketing wants," Brad said lamely.

"You know," Jim said slowly, "I'm told engineers prize their independence and their creativity. But this lab has neither. You're in thrall to other people's schedules. And you have very little time for creativity if you're spending most of your time waiting for information."

It was a moment before Brad replied. "Well, I suppose that's part of being an engineer. You make an informed guess, then you see if you guessed right. We often do, you know." Pride appeared on Brad's face: the pride of a person who had worked his way through engineering school and was very protective of his status.

"I don't doubt it. But you still have to wait for confirmation that your guess was right. Then if it isn't, you have to do that work over again. Not the best use of your expensive qualifications. Look," Jim went on, "I want to start treating some of the processes that go on in this lab the same way that we do manufacturing processes. I think it might release you engineers, and the support staff, for better things in the long run. Waiting around or redoing work that's been done on the basis of insufficient information is a waste of your time."

"Jim, please understand. As I said before, we're not machines. And we don't work like production workers. The time it takes is not the point. The important thing is the caliber of what comes out."

"But Brad, you have to admit it's not coming out."

"I don't agree. This lab has a long history of designing great products. But marketing has been putting out unrealistic dates. If anything, we need more people, and less pushing from marketing and corporate."

Jim sighed. He knew that if things worked as he intended, fewer people would be needed, not more. "Brad, I'd like to see your schedule for the YR3 computer," Jim said, getting up and moving over to peer at some charts on the wall.

"That's so far out of date, it's not even close anymore," Brad said.

Jim thought he detected a trace of anger in Brad's voice.

"Let's get it up to date then, and measure how well we comply with the schedule. I'd also like to find out how much time everyone spends in meetings."

Brad frowned. "What d'you mean?"

"Everyone should keep track of the meetings they attend: what they're about, who they're with, and how long they last."

Brad looked exasperated. "Lots are called on the spur of the moment."

"Then keep two lists. One for scheduled meetings with forty-eight hours notice. Note down who called it, whether there's an agenda, what role the individual played, and afterwards, whether it led to necessary changes. The second list should keep track of all meetings that last more than ten minutes, and have less than forty-eight hours notice."

"Some are just phone calls," Brad objected.

"Fine. Telephone calls, too."

"Aren't we getting a bit close to a Big Brother scenario? Surveillance and so on," Brad said sarcastically.

"No, because everyone will be gathering their own information. There's nothing undercover going on here. I don't intend to have your telephones tapped." Jim attempted to smile, but the response was stoney. Part of him felt as treacherous as a mole, in spite of his growing conviction that his work was a medicine they had to take if they were going to survive.

"Look, Brad," he added. "We need to get the YR3 out. Nobody is working on it now, you saw that yourself. It's my job to make sure these people are not waiting pointlessly. If we can cut down on waiting time and meeting time, people will have more time to do the work they were trained to do."

***

Walking through Yarrow's plush lobby six weeks later, Jim cursed under his breath. It was unlike him to look back, but he was beginning to wonder if he'd made the wrong decision. His first instincts were always the right ones, yet he'd allowed himself to be conned by Trevor's flattery into taking on an impossible job.

He was angry. Angry with himself, with Trevor, and with the guys in the lab who were making his life a daily misery. His wife, Sally, who had suggested he sit it out, was the only one he didn't feel angry with. He didn't like her advice, but he was hardly in a position to reject it at the moment. After all, he couldn't return to the perfectly satisfactory job he had left.

Walking into the product development lab didn't help. He could feel the hostility blasting up at him as he passed each desk, like barrages of cold air. On the walls hung neat charts, on which individuals had been plotting their time, at his instigation.

Today the information was to be collected, and he was to find out, once and for all, why this talent-packed product development lab was so unproductive.

Jim and Brad didn't find time to begin the analysis until five-thirty that afternoon. Wearily, over the next couple of hours, they plotted the data from the charts. When Brad left, a little after seven o'clock, Jim was too deeply into the data to stop. He phoned Sally and told her he'd be working late. He was beginning to see a repeated pattern and wanted to pursue it till he caught and landed his prey.

Two hours later, a telling picture was staring up from his desk. A laugh (the first for some time) escaped him as he looked at it. The picture the graph conjured up was of an almost classic bottleneck. But instead of parts trying to get through a machine, it was dozens of engineers and CAD-CAM operators all trying to lay claim to too few CAD equipment stations.

According to the data, most of the engineers' time was spent in meetings trying to establish who had priority. When any one individual did get to use the equipment, it was often not for long. The overloading of individuals with projects was partly a result of this. People took on more so they would not have time on their hands as they waited to get to the CAD equipment to work on their main projects.

The result was that nobody was spending much time on any one project. A lot of people had three projects going at once and were scheduled to be working on all of them full-time. One engineer had eight projects. It was sheer chaos. Each of these projects required extensive time in communications with other people on the project. The net result was a continuous stream of meetings, and very little time spent on the projects themselves.

This was evidence enough to be going on. At nine-thirty, Jim put away his work. He would have something to tell Brad tomorrow. He still felt like a spy, but now he felt like a successful one. And maybe his spy master wasn't so wrong about the importance of the operation after all.

When Brad appeared next morning, Jim showed him the graphs with something verging on excitement.

"Brad, in light of this, we're going to make some changes," he began. "Clearly, our first priority is to get out the YR3. So, we're going to put a halt on all products except that and two others." Brad's face froze. "That way you'll have enough CAD equipment to handle them all."

Brad faced him with a disbelieving smile. "That's impossible. People won't have anything to do." He shook his head, and Jim wished he didn't have to give the man so much stress.

"I know, it takes getting used to," he said. "But it'll happen naturally if things go according to plan."

"What's this plan?" Brad looked as if he was about to have something hurled at him a second time.

"We're going to stop asking people to do two hundred fifty percent of what they're capable of doing," said Jim evenly. "It's counterproductive. People are chronically over-scheduled in this lab."

"That's nothing unusual," said Brad. "Everyone's under pressure, all over the company."

"Yes, but being under pressure is severely damaging our ability to produce. I propose that we examine every project. Our aim is to find out whether we're working around missing people, or at least their missing time."

Brad raised his eyebrows quizzically. "I'm not sure I follow you."

"I'll give you an example. If someone is supposed to spend twenty-five percent of his time on a project and he doesn't manage more than ten percent because of pressure from elsewhere, we stop the project altogether. If three people are supposed to work on a project and only two of them are available, we stop that project, too."

"This is going to mean major reorganization," said Brad almost under his breath.

"Not necessarily. At some point, we either redo the schedule, or find people who can give the project their undivided time and attention. If we don't," he said, his voice growing more emphatic, "too many of these projects will be stretched out till they no longer have any value."

"You're talking about losing some people, aren't you?" Brad said, sounding so unhappy that Jim silently berated himself for failing to see one of the central problems from Brad's point of view. Brad's empire would shrink: a blow to him, and a worry too. He was concerned about the well-being of the lab people.

"I don't expect to get rid of anyone," Jim replied. "Once we've got things organized so that no one is working around missing resources, we'll assign them all back their jobs, but this time in such a way that they can pay full attention to them."

"And what will they do until then?"

"We'll teach them process control," Jim replied. He was beginning to enjoy himself. "It doesn't do any good to have people creating PC boards that can't be designed, or that have to be changed later. That's no better use of their time, is it?"

Brad looked as if he might implode.

***

"So?" Trevor Leonis was looking stronger and more certain of himself than ever as Jim confronted him across his desk ten days later.

"I've found out a heck of a lot." Jim let a small sheaf of papers land on the desk between them, like a peace offering. "I'd like to see what you think."

For three or four long minutes, Trevor thumbed through the pile. Every now and again, he let out a grunt, whether of approval or dissatisfaction, Jim wasn't sure. Then he looked up.

"Good, good. Just what I was hoping for. Just what I suspected. So tell me your plan."

"Well, the most obvious problem is one I'm very familiar with: 'working around.' In this case, working around missing information. The engineers have designed the central processor board eight times, and built three prototypes. They're still making changes to the specs."

"From what I see here, there's also an overload of designs going through."

"True. There's a severe bottleneck at the CAD workstations. Everything, including the YR3, marks time waiting for its turn. When they get there, they don't get enough time."

"Why don't we expand the CAD operation so it doesn't cause a bottleneck?"

"Why do that?" asked Jim. "Bottlenecks are useful in any system. We use them to regulate what we do. If we expand the CAD workstations, bottlenecks will still happen; they'll just get pushed downstream."

"So you end up chasing bottlenecks and trying to unplug them all over the shop. Sounds uncomfortable. Almost as bad as Mr. Roto-Rooter's job."

"You're right," said Jim, who appreciated Trevor's occasional indulgence in silly remarks. "It's better to have a controlled bottleneck, in a location where we expect it. By allowing too many projects into the system at once, we get all sorts of complexities down the line. If we keep CAD capacity limited, it acts as a kind of gatekeeper. Once we've got the flow controlled, we can start adding capacity once again."

"So what else, Jim?" Trevor leaned back and regarded him with interest.

"I want to be sure that CAD operators have all the information they need before they start working. I won't buy any more CAD equipment until I'm sure they're not working around missing information."

"You always were the conservative type, Jim," chuckled Trevor. "So when's your plan going to hit the fan?"

Jim looked surprised. "It's already hit. You haven't heard the explosion?"

Trevor leaned forward, a look of relish appearing on his face. "No, I've been out of town."

"Go check your electronic mail. You'll find out there." He paused, then laughed. "Well, I won't hold you in suspense. We picked out three projects, including the YR3, of course, and we've put all the others on hold. We're going to release new products only as CAD capacity exists, and if the information to do the project is complete."

Trevor looked contemplative, though a small frown had appeared between his eyebrows.

"Trevor," Jim cautioned him, "I don't need your doubts. Just look at the facts. Every product we've delivered to manufacturing has been redesigned six to ten times. These engineers are addicted to redesign. The CAD is a toy they can't resist."

"The search for perfection can't hold up production," Trevor intoned.

"Marketing is looking for perfection too. Much of the impetus to keep redesigning comes from them. So we've had to come up with a firm solution. We're not going to spend time building products until it's been firmly decided exactly what they'll be. Any changes after that come out as the next generation of the product."

"I never knew you could be so radical, Jim," said Trevor. He was holding his pen up close in front of his face, and staring at it. The effect on his eyes gave him a slightly unnerving look. "Remember, we're trying to move from one generation of computers to the next. Rollover is a perilous time for a company. Some have been bankrupted by it. Yarrow may need all the products it can muster to stay afloat."

Jim decided to come on strong. "In my opinion, most companies are putting out too many different types of products, and this weakens them. Their resources are fragmented. Products that come out in shotgun response to a short-term market demand will not be the best. It's better to pick a few products with the greatest potential and let them evolve to be the best on the market."

Trevor was still looking at his pen. Jim started feeling defensive, but then corrected himself. "For too long Yarrow has been puttering around, making dozens of inconsequential items which keep the work force busy, and keep the company's name out there. It's time we chuck all that, and go for top prize."

Trevor moved his pen from its guard position in front of his nose, and contemplatively placed the end of it into his mouth. Rather tensely he said, "I put you in charge, Jim. Go for it."

***

The time period during rollover from the YR2 to the YR3 tested his theories to the utmost, as Jim knew it would. There were days when he felt like a pilot trying to land a jumbo jet without hydraulics. But he stuck to the rule book and kept his crew calm as they made the transition.

A few weeks after the new schedule started, there was a major fracas between marketing and the product development lab. The question was the launch date of the YR3, which had been brought forward dramatically: eleven months reduced to four.

The marketing department, which had counted on a distant date for the appearance of its biggest star, was scrambling to get its own schedule in line with the lab's. Based on observations of past performance, some of the staff were also unwilling to believe that the lab would keep to this commitment.

Manufacturing was also having difficulty bringing its schedule in sync with the new rhythms. Purchasing was worried about ordering too few supplies for the old product before the new one was ready to go, or alternatively overbuying for the new version of the YR computer until they were sure of their production figures.

"This is a headache," Greg Turner, the chief buyer, confessed to Jim, grasping his bald patch in a gesture of exasperation. "My process control will go to the dogs if I don't get more information from the lab and from manufacturing. But nobody can agree on plausible dates for this YR3 to go into production. I'm going to end up with too much inventory or not enough, unless something changes."

Jim called a meeting the following week to try to resolve this new slew of problems. It lasted almost all day, but a simple and useful concept came out of it. At the end of the meeting, most people went home tired but elated. Later, Jim sat at the kitchen table with his wife, Sally, replaying the events of the day.

"We've won some battles decisively," he said as his cat settled on his lap. "Everyone has accepted that manufacturing's involvement at the design stage is essential. There'd been some dispute about exactly when they should come in. But today we agreed that an assembler should be part of each design team."

"They'll keep the engineers focused on what's feasible, I suppose," put in Sally.

"What's feasible, yes. But they'll also keep watching for design features that might cause problems when the product is in production. They'll help find ways to avoid unnecessary complications. We need designs which offer the fewest possible opportunities for defects." He paused and stroked the circle of orange and black fur on his lap, as it vibrated with contented purrs. "It's surprising how many companies use quality engineers instead of process control. We're going to try to avoid that."

Sally looked surprised. "But surely, the quality engineer is the one who does the process control?"

"That's true, up to a point. But he's there in addition to constant process control. If problems aren't caught, or prevented from arising at an early stage, thousands of hours could be wasted by the time the quality engineer pounces on them. At the moment, we're using our quality engineers instead of process control. They roll up their sleeves when the product rolls off the line."

"You're talking about changing mindsets here," said Sally, who was concocting an elaborate fruit salad for an event the following day.

"You're absolutely right," said Jim. "Engineers, for example, feel that if they can diagram something in a complete enough way, by definition the product will work. They don't always take into account the real world, which can be very different from even the best of models. Information from marketing, for instance, should be as complete as information from manufacturing. Engineers have to be sensitive to customer quirks, changing costs, all the practical realities of manufacturing. Remember I told you about Sue Garrish?"

"Yes, of course. Marketing manager, isn't she?"

"Right, and a very hard-headed person, too. Well, she stood up today and gave what amounted to a speech. She actually said she was thrilled by the changes that had been taking place. She was so fired up that some people applauded!"

Sally smiled. "So someone's pleased, then?"

"Well, more than just Sue, I think," Jim said modestly. "Even I'm surprised. A month or so ago, for example, marketing and design engineers were spending most of their meetings griping at each other. Then things suddenly changed, according to Sue. She told us the lab people became impossible to ignore because they all had grins on their faces." Sally laughed, and held out a piece of cantaloupe to Jim on the end of a fork. "Apparently the mood was contagious. The changes spread informally, with people telling each other what had happened in their departments over beers after work and at lunch—you know the kind of thing. Everybody wants to get in on the act and find out how to get the same kind of thing going in their own departments."

"A real success story," commented Sally, coming around the table and kissing Jim on top of the head.

"Well, it happened almost by itself, to tell the truth. People in other departments started to realize they were battling with some of the same problems as the product design lab. Habits like working around missing items, information, or materials are very common, though most people think it's a little disease that shows up only in manufacturing. Anyway, there was still a problem about agreeing to production times. So Greg Turner came up with the idea of creating a task schedule that would be as irrevocable as tooling."

"You've lost me," said Sally.

"Well, departments tend to create their own schedules, and then keep adjusting them to try and coincide with one another. It causes a lot of bad feeling and wasted time because everything keeps shifting. These changing schedules are disastrous for the purchasing department, and also for marketing, if they've booked ad space, for example, or planned a launch and then the product isn't ready. We're talking about thousands of dollars here—sometimes more."

"So this master schedule has to be 'set in concrete'—not just a piece of paper," said Sally.

"Right. Everyone has to stick with it. If something goes wrong in one department and people can't fulfill their obligations, everything comes to a complete halt until they can get back on track. If the errors build up to a point where no one can make headway, the master schedule coordinator has to redo it. But we'll keep working to get more and more accurate compliance with the schedule as it is. And the basic principle remains: Once the schedule is agreed on, no one messes with it."

"That sounds awfully radical, Jim. You look fierce," Sally said, glancing at him in surprise. "Are you always like that at work?"

"Trevor said almost the same thing," Jim replied. "I'm beginning to think I must be."

***

Brad couldn't suppress the beam on his face. "The modem design was completed and signed off yesterday. Manufacturing knows about it in detail, and they don't foresee any problems."

It had been three months since Jim's scheme had gone into effect. The YR3 was on the verge of rolling down the production line. The lab was buzzing. "Looks as if you're having no trouble keeping people occupied," commented Jim with a sly smile.

"Well, they may be working fewer hours," Brad replied, ignoring the implied reference to his earlier disbelief. "But they're doing a far better job. The time going into all that brainstorming at the beginning has been healthy for the products and the people."

"Things are beginning to roll, Brad. But we can't stop here. Now that we have more time to use constructively, we have to start rooting out other complexities."

"Burn-in," said Brad. "That's one of them. I've got some ideas for making it a more useful operation."

"Oh?"

"Currently we're testing every product," Brad continued heatedly, "and we replace parts that don't stand up to the heat."

"Right."

"This seems like a real waste of resources to me. One of the technicians working at the ovens pointed out that the same faults are coming up time after time."

"He's right," Jim agreed. "The burn-in process has always been unsatisfactory."

"It's not just that testing every product seems darned wasteful," Brad went on, unstoppable. "It's that taking out the weak parts and replacing them usually doesn't even solve the problem. The so-called corrected products are another hotbed of defects." He looked at Jim inquiringly. Jim looked back, trying to conceal his incredulity at the way this man had changed. "The point being that about ninety percent of the parts we pull are still good," Brad finished.

"So, it's a case of redesigning the circuits, not the parts themselves. Interesting point, Brad. I can see there'll be no resting on our laurels around here."

"You said it yourself, Jim," Brad grinned. "Doing well is okay, but doing better is . . . well, a whole lot better!"

Several months later, sitting one Saturday evening on Trevor's back patio, watching their teenagers dive and horse around in the pool, Jim said, "You know, I have to give you credit, Trevor. You have a lot more faith in what's possible than I do. I admit I'm surprised by how this has all turned out."

"I have more faith in you than you do yourself, that's the truth," replied Trevor, pushing the salted nuts towards him. "We both know that almost anything's possible once you start reducing complexity. We've both done it before. And it's normal to accomplish more than you had planned."

Jim chuckled. "But you know, one thing happened that I really didn't foresee. This purge of complexity in the lab has shown up a lot of people in their true colors."

"Oh? What d'you mean?" Trevor got up and lifted the lid of the barbecue.

"You know how a lot of the engineers got very crabby about applying process control to their work? They felt it was too tough on their creativity."

"Surely that's a common objection in these rarified circles." Trevor methodically turned the browning pieces of chicken over the coals.

"Well, it turns out that even with the snarl-ups removed, some of these engineers are really not very creative. They're just journeymen, but we never had the opportunity to discern it before. A couple of others who were doing routine work have come up with great ideas since they've been relieved of more mundane duties. It's interesting."

"So you've been doing some reshuffling of jobs?" Trevor inquired.

"As tactfully as we can. Some people always feared that the changes would be a threat to them. I suppose it's been true, in a way. But we've tried to upset people as little as possible."

"Good. So what would you say has been the biggest benefit of all this?"

Jim sniffed appreciatively at the mesquite-scented air wafting his way. "Mmmmm, those smell good. Biggest benefit? For me, it's all those bright faces coming through the door in the mornings. For them, it's that they get off at a reasonable hour in the evenings, and they worry less."

"And for the company?"

"Well, shucks, I almost forgot about the company!" Jim laughed. "The changes are coming so fast I hardly recognize it for what it was. Did I tell you about the burn-in program?"

"No."

"When people from the lab got talking to manufacturing, they realized that a major part of their time was dedicated to burn-in. By this time, the lab people were in a position to take on a challenge or two. So they used statistics to find out what weaknesses the burn-in process was showing. On the basis of those results, they decided to make some design changes to increase the reliability of the product."

"Good, good . . ." Trevor appeared to be drifting off a little, as he stared contentedly into the dusk.

"Get to the point, Jim," came Sally's voice, laughing as she dumped bowls of tortilla chips and salsa onto the table behind them. "We need your help around here."

"Well, the upshot is," Jim paused as he reached around to grab a chip, "that we're only screening ten percent of the computers, instead of doing the customary burn-in of every item."

Trevor uncoiled like a spring as he looked around at Jim. "You've just saved us the cost of building another plant!"

Jim crunched on chips, smiling. "Well, I liked the concept."

"Hey, I'm absolutely serious. The cost of burn-in is tremendous, and on the whole it's a wasted effort. Even when the weak links are flushed out, replacing those parts has never been a satisfactory solution. Any other pleasant surprises?"

"We have custom designs on the drawing board for at least six specialist markets," said Jim, hoisting the bowl of chips off the table and holding them out to Trevor. "We've got special keyboards for three foreign countries. We've got one version of the YR3 for the intelligence community and another for insurance. The potential for niche markets is endless."

"Why not? The YR3 is the best in its class."

"But, Trevor, we couldn't even get this gizmo finished eight months ago. Now we're doing variations on it. That should double our market, at least."

"That flexibility should translate into more frequent updates too. Tell me how you did it."

"Well, in a sense, we've become more flexible because we've become more rigid," said Jim.

"Have I got to solve a paradox now?" asked Trevor, with a mock groan. "Jim, I'm supposed to be relaxing."

"No, I'm serious. One of the reasons we were in a mess was that the schedules for the different departments—marketing, purchasing, manufacturing, and product design—were just not corresponding. Every time a small change was made in one, all the others were thrown out of whack. The adjustments were costing a fortune. They were also a major reason for all the holdups."

"So, what have you done?"

"We've made the ultimate schedule, and we all use it, regardless of individual fluctuations. We regard the schedule as unchangeable as tooling. No one messes with it."

"That's a very sensible analogy," Trevor commented, nodding slowly. "Ninety-nine percent of our talk on quality issues is about hard quality: that is, defect rates, cycle times, and so on. So most of our process control concepts apply only to hard quality issues."

"True. Yet material flow is even more important, and forecasting and product development still more. You can't forecast without a product development cycle that you have some trust in. The buyers can't buy unless they have a firm idea of the forecast. And it makes little sense for manufacturing to worry about hard quality issues if they have no material . . ."

". . . So, from now on, the schedule becomes the quality master!" interjected Trevor. He raised his voice and bellowed into the evening air, "Kids! Come get your grub!"

As dripping bodies hauled themselves out of the pool, the conversation turned to other things. But, looking at his family and friends through the warm dusk, Jim felt a modest sense of pride in the accomplishments of the past few months. He could never say he had achieved everything he wanted to. That was not in the nature of the work he had chosen. As far as he was concerned, no more room for improvement was a contradiction in terms. But for now, he felt like a man who had earned his leisure.

***

LESSONS FROM THE ENGINEER'S STORY

Excess Complexity Hurts Every System in a Company

This story shows how the same issues that are important in manufacturing crop up in "soft" quality areas: product development, marketing, sales, and others. Having a system and trying to remove complexity in these areas can boost productivity in product development three to five times, as Jim shows Brad and the others.

The Product as a Work of Art

At Yarrow, lack of products is not the problem in product development. Working on too many products is the problem. Engineers are designing too many irrelevant products, and are reworking designs too often, in search of perfection. The engineers also try to control all randomness by making endless corrections. The department has lost touch with its mission: to create commercial products that will sell and yield a reasonable profit.

The approach of designing the product as a work of art, combined with the Christmas tree syndrome (everyone must have his or her ornament on it) ignores the life cycle of the product, so that opportunities are lost. Both the engineering and marketing function at Yarrow fall victim to this behavior. This phenomenon, also known as "creeping elegance," holds up production.

In his initial discussion with Jim, Brad does not understand that all the rework is unnecessary and counterproductive. People are doing their best, but complexity in the system thwarts them.

The engineers have responded to the situation by creating work to remain busy, but "busyness" is not productivity. They are also resigned to, and almost proud of, trying to operate without the information they need.

This results in the major scheduling inconsistencies that Jim points out, as well as lost profit opportunities, as the sales of the YR2 languish. The YR3, a crucial product, could really be ready for production in two months if all the necessary information were available. But, because people's mindsets are geared to assuming long cycles of design changes, this product has been scheduled for release more than a year in the future. These kinds of delays make rollover, the transition from the existing product to its replacement, an extremely perilous time for the company.

For Discussion:

✓   How do the problems in Yarrow's "soft" quality areas affect its "hard" quality systems?

The Role of Information

Jim, as an outsider, brings a fresh outlook because he does not assume that change is impossible. His strong background in improving productivity in "hard" quality (manufacturing) can be applied to the product development lab. Jim understands that product development cycle times must be reduced if the company is to get through the rollover period successfully and remain profitable. This can be done only if all parties—engineering, manufacturing, marketing—are brought together at the outset so that the maximum amount of information is available early in the project.

More information also means fewer flaws in the system and better products because engineers will have more time to brainstorm at the beginning of the design stage. Jim knows that engineers at Yarrow are working around missing resources: information crucial to them. This is a major cause of the complexity in the product development system. It creates the engineering equivalent of WIP (work in process), as unfinished projects linger on the drawing boards.

By having people keep track of meetings, Jim discovers that the engineers are spending inordinate amounts of time communicating information and debating the scheduling of their (too) many projects, and therefore, do not have enough time to work on the projects themselves. Marketing aggravates the situation by continually changing the product requirements and causing more rework.

The final solution is that everyone gets as much information as possible, as early as possible, and that engineering will not build products until all requirements are determined. Any changes after this time will be reflected later in a new version of the product.

> **For Discussion:** Think about the conditions necessary for having Jim's solution work at Yarrow.
>
> ✓   How does this change the nature of how departments work together?

The Schedule Battle

The scheduling system at Yarrow has lost touch with reality, and both the marketing and engineering departments are unrealistic in what they expect. The problem has two aspects. First, there is a lack of understanding about how to allocate people's time to get the work done. Second, the schedule itself is incorrect because of assumptions about design changes and missing information.

In addressing the schedule's actual time frame, Jim must see that the engineers stop building in time for changes and stop constantly reworking designs: two factors that have made schedules much longer than they need to be. This almost inevitably means that marketing, purchasing, and other departments must cooperate in defining project requirements at the outset and not make unnecessary changes. In effect, the product development schedule becomes part of a rigid master schedule, which is not to be violated lightly.

In order for Jim and the others to allocate people's time

accurately, the bottleneck in the product development system must be found.

For Discussion:
✓   How can a rigid schedule actually give a company more flexibility and leverage?
✓   What must the departments in a company do before they can agree on a valid master schedule?

Finding the Bottleneck and Balancing Work Flow

Jim institutes a process of data collection to locate the bottlenecks, over the resistance of Brad and the others, who want to clean things up before taking data. The bottleneck turns out to be, interestingly enough, a service function: too few workstations on the CAD system. This bottleneck causes people to argue and spend time trying to schedule their projects, and gives them the incentive to create new projects with which to keep busy when their original ones become stuck in the CAD system.

The solution appears counterintuitive to most people in the American corporate structure. The department must avoid overloading the system. Engineers must limit the amount of work and focus completely on the important projects, even if it means that people temporarily may have nothing to do. Brad is flabbergasted by this solution, but Jim's background has taught him that it is better to do nothing at all than to do things that are counterproductive.

These actions will create a linear, balanced flow of work through the department, unlike working around missing information or overscheduling people, both of which make problems worse. Work will be released from the CAD system only if it is complete and correct. This will reduce flaws later on. Now the company can cope with the rollover period because what is important will get done, and everyone can have confidence in the products. Yarrow and its engineers will enjoy profitable returns on their efforts.

For Discussion: On the surface, simply expanding the CAD operation may appear more logical and easier than what Jim does.

✓   Why is Jim's solution ultimately better?
✓   What do you think would happen if the bottle-neck were removed?

4

THE WORKER'S STORY
Questioning Old Habits

IN THE CAFETERIA of the Murrow Reeves Company, workers stood about, leaning against tables, joking together in groups or staring ahead with vaguely anxious looks on their faces. The faint aroma of fried potatoes seemed to give the expected arrival of the manufacturing manager an air of déjà vu: yesterday's lunch accompanied by tired old complaints about the failure of the department to reach its shipping quota.

To George Lotis, a recent arrival on the production line, the scene was not so tedious. He had not yet experienced a "Vince Lombardi speech" from the manager, and he welcomed the opportunity to escape from his workstation for twenty minutes. As a newcomer at Murrow Reeves, he was curious to get a sense of the size of the company: about one hundred fifty people in manufacturing alone, he judged from the people still plodding in through the door.

Mr. Baddeley, the manufacturing manager, swept in and took the stage, which was the area in front of the serving hatch. His brow looked slightly furrowed above his red striped tie and impeccable pale gray suit. He began without ceremony. "The news is not so good, folks. We're running behind by almost thirty percent of our shipping schedule this month. We were twenty-seven percent behind at the same time last month, so we're getting worse, not better."

"Same old story," muttered someone behind George.

"On top of this, our labor variance shows we're not controlling our costs. Our only option is to ask for a fifty percent increase in output during the last week of this month. That means each and every one of you will have to exceed your quota by fifty percent."

George, who had had trouble making three-quarters of his quota, glanced guiltily to his right. He almost wondered if anyone were fixing an accusing eye on him. Was he the source of their worsening figures, he thought, as he felt small beads of sweat start to roll down under his collar?

"Not only that, but we're receiving more complaints from customers," Baddeley droned on. "Customer service has reported a twelve percent increase in returns and complaints about poor quality.

"Management has made a big push to improve the quality of this company's goods. We've learned new techniques, tried to educate you guys and put in more quality inspectors. But all this is going to be useless unless you do your part. I know—we all know—that you're good people and you work hard. And we appreciate your efforts. But you're going to have to do even better. We know we're doing our stuff. You just have to do yours, too. I want everyone to pay extra attention to what they're doing. You're going to have to put your lives on hold next week and give any extra time you can manage to the company. Everyone will have to do some overtime. . . ."

Small groans erupted as the group filed out of the cafeteria. Looking at their backs, George was reminded of a herd of elephants: a bit slow, reluctant to move, and with that saggy look that people acquire when they're dispirited.

George went back to his station. As one of the assemblers, he had to put together a computer terminal from a kit of about two hundred parts. He had always been the mechanically minded one at home. Everyone called on him to fix their television sets, take their toasters apart, and look into their car engines. The assembly of this terminal would have been no big deal if it weren't for two major hitches that kept cramping his style.

Often, his kit arrived with parts missing. He would build the terminal as far as he could. Then he had to decide whether to put it to one side and wait, which meant a couple of hours' work were discounted for that day. Or, he could scramble around trying to get the missing part from somewhere else. Sometimes, he would vandalize one of his own completed terminals, put the part in for size, finish building the rest of it, then take out the part and replace it in the first terminal.

George hated doing this. It was a mess, and often both terminals were returned from inspection anyway. Juggling parts like this just didn't seem to work.

The other problem was worse, because it happened on every single terminal. The magnet, or yoke as it was commonly called, did not fit correctly around the cathode ray tube. Every time he got to that part of the assembly, his work came to a standstill: like the half-finished job sitting in front of him now.

He had tried fitting the yoke a number of different ways, but that one piece usually took as much time as all the rest of the pieces put together. To make things worse, he sometimes had to take the yoke back out after testing because it needed minor repair, like the time the wires had been crossed the wrong way.

George decided he had better swallow his pride and ask his supervisor how best to get the yoke on. Les, a quiet man who never said much, came over and worked with him. While Les worked, he pointed out a few other common pitfalls that led to defects.

"You gotta pincushion the thing this way so you get a picture that fills up the screen," he said, manipulating the awkward thing. "Keep moving and stretching the yoke till you get the right picture. This creates the magnetic field that adjusts the beam, so it has to be done right."

George could see that Les was having some difficulty with the yoke himself. When he finally was ready to send the completed terminal off to inspection, George had a strong feeling it wasn't right. But since his supervisor had assembled it, he decided to send it with crossed fingers anyway. He didn't intend to go through that hassle again.

Conversation was subdued at lunchtime, with people speculating about the company's troubles and the possibility of layoffs if things didn't improve. George took the opportunity to talk with a guy he had nodded to a few times. He was about twenty-two, close to George's age; not one of the old-timers who never talked except to give advice.

Sitting out in the back, George decided to tell him what was going on. "Been here long?" he asked.

"Five months," answered the other, whose name was Mike.

"Like it?"

"It's okay. Money could be better."

George took the plunge. "You can say that again. I'm getting little enough because I'm still in training. Trouble is, at this rate, I may never get out. I'm usually good at assembly, but some of the parts in these kits stink."

"Right," replied Mike offhandedly, taking a bite out of his pastrami sandwich.

"Right?" George was surprised at his unconcerned tone. "You don't sound worried. What the heck do you do about parts that don't fit and hold up your work?"

"Yeah, you mean the yokes. There's been problems with those things for as long as I've been here. Everybody knows they stink. There are a few tricks some of the guys have developed. You won't get them to tell what they are, though. Nobody wants to give up their place in the ranking." He laughed humorlessly.

George wondered how aggressive he should be in his questioning. "D'you have a trick?" he asked after a pause.

Mike grinned. "Not exactly. But I stashed away a few yokes made by a different manufacturer when they came around last time. They're a different color. Work ten times better. I use them when I'm really under the gun."

"You mean those rotten gray things are not the only ones?"

"For us they are, at least most of the time. Purchasing buys them because they can get them at the best price. They don't care if we lose time working on them."

So rotten parts were screwing up the whole system, thought George, as his temper started to rise. We're spending all this time trying to work with bad parts, and it's keeping us from making really first-class terminals. It's also slowing us down. And since everyone wants to keep a high ranking, nobody is willing to help anyone. With a mess like this, there's sure not going to be any cooperation!

As he worked on through the afternoon, George resolved to get to the bottom of this mystery. He felt so crazy, he sometimes wanted to throw a terminal on the floor and kick it, like a child knocking down a house of blocks. But being turned back into a child was not what he had expected of this job. He had arrived with hopes of doing well and moving on to better things. George had recently started to face the fact that he'd been an irresponsible loafer for a long time, flunking exams at school and taking life as a bit of a joke. But things had changed in the past year. He had met a girl who seemed unlike the rest, and he was willing to do anything to win her. Instead, he was getting nowhere. Not only that, but he was beginning to fear that this one diabolical part might cost him his job. Even though he was starting to hate his work, he couldn't afford to be laid off.

Yet it was already becoming clear that this wasn't a simple matter of personal frustration. The more he thought about it, the more the whole situation looked like a house of cards with a bent card stuck somewhere in the middle. For the sake of one bad card, the whole structure was tumbling down.

George almost wanted to stay late that day and try to find out more about what was going on. But he'd promised Laura he would take her to a movie, so he left at the usual time. Compulsory overtime was to begin on Monday. He was beginning to think he might have to do some voluntary overtime too, just to keep his job. One way or another, this might be the last opportunity for an evening out for a while.

***

Even with the antics of a macho brute in a futuristic America to distract him, George wasn't having fun as he sat in the dark movie theater. He felt more like someone trapped in a mine elevator, unable to move either up or down and in grave danger of an explosion right under him.

Later, over beer and pizza, George was almost silent.

"You normally reinvent the plot after a movie," Laura said. "What's up? You seem so gloomy."

George took a large gulp of beer. "It's going to be a while before I get rich on this job, Laura. I don't know whether to pack it in, or hang on and hope things get better. Trouble is, companies have been laying people off. It wouldn't be that easy to get another job."

"So what's the problem?" asked Laura, who always went straight to the heart of the matter. "When you went for the interview it sounded as if the job would pay well."

"It did," George hated to admit the truth. "But I'm not even doing well enough to get off my training wage. It sounds crazy, but the materials are just not working together." He tried to explain the problem of the yoke, and the peculiar conspiracy of silence that seemed to surround everyone's difficulties with the part.

Laura thought for a moment, then asked, "Isn't there some way you could get a different yoke that works better?" she asked.

George guffawed sarcastically. "Boy, you're innocent. D'you think I can start ordering the materials manager around when I only got there a few weeks ago? If I'd been there ten years I wouldn't have a say on parts."

That silenced Laura, but not for long. After discussing the coming weekend and plans to go fishing, she remarked, "I don't see why."

"You don't see why what?"

"Why you can't tell the materials manager what's happening. They're never going to know you're a good worker if you stay in this situation. It's not fair to you. It's not fair to the company."

George started to pick up the last slice of pizza, then put it down again. "What d'you mean, not fair to the company?"

"Look, George, you're wasting company time messing around with bad parts that don't fit. It's causing trouble all over the department. Wouldn't it be better for them to look for a different supplier?"

George looked stunned for a moment. He had always admired Laura's directness. But she was talking like a free human being. That was the way he used to feel. This job had cowed him more than he realized. He had let himself slide into the position of underdog without even noticing it. For the first time in his life, he felt completely powerless, and he hated it. He was getting really depressed.

"They don't listen to people like me, Laura. If I make a nuisance of myself, they'll say I'm not trainable. As far as they're concerned, if I make suggestions, it looks like criticism. If I criticize, they'll say I'm not part of the team—and that means doing what I'm told like a good boy, without complaining."

"But use your head, George. I'm talking common sense," said Laura, the flush of battle appearing in her cheeks. "If you're spending all your time fighting with that dumb part, it's got to be costing the company money. Speak up! If this goes on, your company's going to be losing a lot more money than they'd ever dream of paying you."

"Well, I certainly have the right to get myself kicked out. That's what speaking up would do for me. D'you think the company really listens to our opinions, Laura? We're told we can make suggestions and complaints if we want to; some kind of new fad they got from Japanese companies, I heard. There are even cartoons on the walls saying, 'Do our ears hang low?' that talk about how everyone is so willing to listen to everyone else." George stared moodily into his empty beer glass.

"But it's like Baddeley, when it comes down to it," he continued. "It's all show. I've been trying to find out what the deal is on those rotten parts for the past month. Other people understand, but they won't tell me. They talk about teamwork, but everyone's out for his own quota. And management wouldn't listen to me if I suggested doing it different. When it comes down to it, they wouldn't take us seriously if we asked for anything more than another roll of toilet paper when it runs out."

"Maybe they need someone to start the ball rolling," Laura said thoughtfully. "Maybe they need someone who can show that you guys have something worth saying. How can their new theory work if nobody tries putting it into practice?"

"What I have to say will sound like a load of trouble to

everyone, except the workers, and even some of them couldn't care less," said George bitterly.

Laura planted her chin in her hands and looked squarely across the table at him. George thought what wonderful eyes she had: as blue as the sparkling swimming pool he wouldn't mind having in their shared backyard one day.

"Look," she said. "Did you ever hear of the girl who cut the ends off the roast?" George kept staring at her eyes. What could meat have to do with anything?

"When someone asked her why, she said it was because her mother always did," Laura continued, undeflected by his dreamy look.

"So?" said George cheerily, thinking about going for another beer.

"When the girl's mother was asked why she cut the ends off, she replied—guess what?—it was because her mother always did."

George yawned. He realized he was very tired.

"Don't go to sleep," Laura said, kicking his foot under the table. "You haven't heard the punch line yet."

"So why?" he asked dutifully.

"Because the grandmother had a tiny roasting pan!"

George laughed. It was true. People would willingly ruin a good thing just because old habits dictated it. But he really paid attention when Laura added, "Anyway, you've never been one to take things lying down. You'll be head of a manufacturing outfit one day and then it'll be your job to make changes. So you might as well start practicing now."

George punched her playfully. "I'm not sure about the roasting pan story, but you've earned your second beer for that."

***

The next day, the terminal Les had worked on with George came back. It had failed inspection. Reason: a problem with the yoke. As he worked it over again, George did some rough figuring. The time wasted in fitting the gray yokes must be costing the company a bundle, even on his hourly wage, which wasn't much. Multiply that by all the other workers struggling for at least half an hour with each one. Add the quality inspectors, who were working overtime catching all those bad apples. On top of that, the returns from dissatisfied customers were costing the company a fortune, and their reputation to boot.

His accuracy might not be perfect, but it was painfully clear that the higher cost of the yoke that worked could hardly match the hidden costs in delays, returns, confusion, and scrap: all caused by the false economy of an inferior part. This didn't even include the invisible costs of stressed, bored, disgusted workers struggling to make their quotas against the odds. George thought about what Laura had said last night. The roasting pan story sounded ridiculous, but maybe she had a point.

He tried once more to bring up the subject with a couple of coworkers, but they changed the subject, or pretended they hadn't heard. As a recent arrival at the company among the veterans who had been there since it began fifteen years before, George knew instinctively that he did not have permission to complain any more than anyone else had the mandate to explain. But he also knew he could do a job well, and the company could be getting the best out of all its workers if only someone would admit what was going on. There was something terribly wrong about this conspiracy of silence.

It was ten more days before George decided to put his security on the line and talk to his supervisor. It had taken one more spur to make him do it, and the spur had come in the form of an article in the local newspaper. Laura had thrown it in front of him after work one day.

"Your company's president should be behind you all the way," she said with a trace of smugness in her voice. "Look at that."

It was a story on the troubles of local companies, and the reasons behind the growing number of layoffs. The president of Murrow Reeves had been asked whether the rumored plans of cutbacks in the work force had any foundation.

"Look at his answer," said George, whistling. "He says, '*We have no plans for layoffs in the foreseeable future. Our new quality program is beginning to show results in many departments, and we are expecting a strong increase in profits in the next quarter. Our teamwork approach is paying off, with greater input from the workers and a real commitment from managers to change at a radical level. I have every faith in the future of Murrow Reeves.'"*

"It's a challenge!" laughed Laura, pounding the table. "Go for it, George!"

***

Les was down by the robots when George next found him alone. He looked worried. The robots were not making the difference everyone had hoped for in the department's speed and efficiency. Instead of simplifying things, they simply added opportunities for holdups.

"Hi, Les, did you see the quote from Mr. Argos in the paper?"

"Somebody told me. I haven't seen it yet though. What's the problem?"

"I need to talk to you about the yokes in these kits. I know it seems like I'm complaining, but I think we need to try a different supplier."

Les looked at him with a wry expression. "And since when have production-line workers been able to dictate to purchasing?" he asked, eyeing a row of packing boxes which the robot was arranging.

"Maybe they need to start now." George heard his own voice echo in his ears as if he had suddenly been transported into a canyon. A deafening silence followed.

"Well, what are you suggesting, exactly?" Les said, still staring at the packing boxes.

"I think someone ought to look into the time being lost fitting the gray yokes. I'm not just trying to save my own skin or reach my own quota, though I wouldn't mind that, I can tell you. When you add up the cost of all the time wasted on these things by all of us, I figure we've got a problem."

Les let out a kind of low growl. George thought he might be clearing his throat to speak. When no comment followed,

George continued, trying to keep the fear out of his voice. "What's the cost of the white yokes I've heard about? I bet we'd save a lot of time with those, even if they are more expensive. It might pay off."

Les was still staring at the rows of boxes. One of the robots suddenly stopped, a box suspended in its claw. "Drat!" he said. But he still stood there, with a look in his eye that could have been growing fury, or growing interest. Suddenly, he turned to George.

"I'll think about it," he said. "But I'm telling you now, I think you're barking up the wrong tree. And now go back to your station. I need to call an engineer to fix this godforsaken machine."

George started to walk back, but then stopped. He turned his head and called over his shoulder, "Les, I think you oughta look at that quote in the paper. It's real interesting."

* * *

The following week was havoc: two to three hours of compulsory overtime every night. Parts ran out. People started hoarding, or even stealing, whatever they could get.

"So this is supposed to be teamwork!" George muttered to Mike as they passed one another one day.

Mike shook his head. "It's every man for himself, pal. I suggest you keep a spare sample of any extra part you can get, and stash them in your locker. Don't let anyone know, though."

Just to get terminals out of his workstation, George would build as far as he could, put in the spare parts so he could test, and then send the terminals on to wait in an area where unfinished terminals were piling up like so many shipwrecks.

Seeing them there depressed George. They were all likely to be duds, even when they did get their missing parts. He knew darned well that when the missing material was put in, his testing of the terminal would no longer mean anything. Yet because of the urgency of making the production target by month's end, quality inspection was letting some of the faulty ones through anyway. This was fine for his quota, but he didn't feel good about the whole picture.

Les didn't refer to their conversation again, but two weeks later, one of the engineers started taking statistics in the computer terminal department. Someone observed while George struggled with the gray yoke. It took exactly forty-three minutes to install, and after testing, took a further twelve minutes of adjustment before the rest of the job could be completed.

George was still not sure, when he sent the terminal out to quality inspection, whether it would hold up under testing there. In spite of his silent elation at what looked like real action on the part of the department manager, he was nervous at being observed so closely. If his terminal came back, it would be noted on records that were seen by more than just the supervisor and the quality manager.

At lunch time, there was a lot of discontented muttering from others about the observation and measurements.

"What's going on?" he asked Mike, feigning innocence.

"For some reason, they want to find out exactly how we're doing with these kits," Mike replied. "Some of the guys are hot about it, I can tell you."

"Why?" George asked. Mike beckoned him outside. He snapped open his can of soda and said, "Some of these guys have found little ways to get their terminals through quality inspection. Their adjustments usually get them that far. But they won't always hold up through packing, transportation, and installation."

"So they don't want anyone taking too close a look at their work," George finished for him. He was praying that nobody had overheard his conversation with Les, aside from the robot. If anyone discovered he was behind this, he would be lynched, he thought grimly. At one point, he had been tempted to tell Mike about his idea, but then decided to use Laura as his sounding board. If she wasn't wiser, she was certainly safer.

The following week, a batch of white yokes arrived: the kind that fit without any trouble. The effect on the department was electric. The fellow next to George hummed loudly as he worked. People talked in the cafeteria instead of muttering.

George's performance started to look more than acceptable. The time he took to install the yoke had gone down to around twelve minutes with three more for adjustment after testing. At this rate, he was finishing as many as five kits a day.

Data was taken again. Crises were less frequent. Backups started to even out. There was even time to get back to the incomplete terminals and finish them properly when a new batch of parts arrived. People could afford the time because they were easily reaching their quotas.

George started feeling good about himself again. He waited for Les to talk to him; to tell him his idea was a good one and it was working out. But no word came. Far from giving him a pat on the back, Les passed him with a deliberate air of avoidance. This discouraged George from asking him what was going on.

Then the gray yokes came back.

George was stunned. It was a blow to everyone in the department. What could have gone wrong? George decided he would have to cut through Les's cold exterior and ask. He waved him down in a corridor one day, like a police car pulling over a speeder.

"Why did they go back to the old yokes, Les? Everything was going great with the new ones."

Les came to a complete halt and addressed George directly for the first time in weeks. "Yes, it was," he said slowly. "I can't tell you all the reasons right now. But, to put it simply, purchasing didn't like the change."

"But that's crazy," countered George. "It's obvious which parts were better."

Les looked reluctant. He glanced along the corridor for a moment, then said in a dramatically lowered voice, "The people in purchasing operate on an incentive system, just like us. They need to get the lowest price they can. Those #!@!* couldn't care less about productivity. They'll never let things change." Considering the mildness of his demeanor, the strength of Les's language came as a surprise.

"But it doesn't make sense. Management keeps talking about workers needing to make more effort, and then they give us parts that screw up our work. Is this some kind of conspiracy, or what?"

"That's the way the system works. Can't do nothing about it." Les nodded with a barely mustered smile and continued on down the corridor.

***

George's pride in his scheme would not allow him to leave it at that. After some soul-searching, he decided to go to talk to the first-line manager, Harold Barr.

Entering Barr's office the next day took the courage of an explorer. The evening before, George and Laura had practiced what he would say. But it was hard to relate his practice interview to the prospect he now faced over the paper-strewn desk of Mr. Barr.

"I want to talk to you for a moment, Mr. Barr. I won't take up much of your time." Barr, a small man with a long strand of hair that he draped carefully over the top of his head to hide his growing bald patch, looked a little surprised.

"Come in," he said. "I have a few minutes. What can I do?" Not having been invited to sit down, George remained standing with his hands tightly clenched behind his back, nervous as a new army recruit.

"About the yokes," he began. A small frown appeared between Barr's eyes. "Well, I wanted to know why we've gone back to the old ones. We were all doing much better with the whites. Not just how much work we got done in a day, but everything seemed to run smoother."

"That may be so," said Barr. "And I appreciate your taking the trouble to come and tell me that. But you know there is more to this question than the number of terminals you get processed, or your morale in the department, even though those things are very important."

Feeling like a second-grader facing the principal, George asked, "What things?" If he was going to take the risk of asking awkward questions, he might as well finish the job, even if it meant burning his bridges with this company altogether. He said, "I'd sure like to know," which added a tinge more respect to his inquiry.

"Well, since you're so interested, you'd better sit down," said Barr. George found himself leveling in more than one sense with the manager, an experience which wasn't as bad as he'd expected. At least he wasn't so distracted by the precariousness of the hair strand from this angle.

"I believe you were the guy who talked to Les about the yokes in the first place, isn't that so? Well, you certainly do have a point. But it's more complicated than it looks. The purchasing department has a bill of materials: a list of standard prices they use to set the price of the finished product. The purchasers are graded, much like you guys are, but in their case, it's on how well they meet those prices.

"The gray yokes you've been using cost considerably less than the white ones. They also help the purchasers balance out overruns or inescapable costs on other parts. People get very upset about purchase price variances, you know. If they can get a really good price on those gray yokes, it could save their skin on a purchase they don't do so well on. And it's all in the company's interest, in the long run."

Almost involuntarily, George felt himself begin to rise out of his chair. "But can't anyone see that using the white yokes would save the company money in the long run? We'd be shipping far more product. I'd be doing more than my quota by now if . . ."

Mr. Barr sighed, as a teacher sighs at a headstrong child. "It's true that the more expensive yoke would probably save money in the long run. But that's not how it would show up in accounting. And that's what counts here."

George felt frustrated. "Thank you, Mr. Barr," he said quietly. Noting to himself that Mr. Barr, whose hair strand was creeping lopsidedly down his forehead, looked like a loser, he turned to walk out the door. But Mr. Barr called him back.

"Don't forget that Mr. Baddeley will be giving a talk to everyone in manufacturing this afternoon. Maybe that will help you feel a little clearer about the way things work here."

The manufacturing manager's speech was essentially the

same one he had given a few weeks before, with the addition of some up-to-date figures about production, which had improved marginally. George even noted that he was wearing the same tie as before, or one very much like it.

But this time George felt no guilt, only disbelief and anger. This speech, more than anything else, made the situation clear to him, but not in the way Mr. Barr had meant.

Since Laura was the only person he felt able to talk to about this, he ventilated some of his feelings that evening, as they walked home after bowling.

"I can't believe they've never noticed these speeches they give us are a complete waste of time."

"Like kids being lectured at school," Laura agreed.

"It's worse than that," said George, "because they're butting their own heads against a brick wall, and teaching us to produce garbage."

Laura glanced at him and took his arm. She wished he wasn't so miserable all the time.

"Don't you see," he went on, "they pretend that motivating us is all they need to do. But how can we be motivated to improve something we have no control over? I'm a trainee worker in a two-tiered wage system: the lowest of the low, in other words. I'm supposed to keep my head down, ask no questions, and make no changes even though I can see the problem more clearly than the managers can. But unless they start opening their eyes and changing the way things work, we'll never be able to speed up, not if they offer us each a Mercedes convertible."

Laura couldn't help smiling at this image. "Why not let them try it anyway?" she joked. "I'd be willing to go along with the plan."

But George was still scowling. "You know, I think they actually cause the problems by refusing to look at the things that are really holding us up."

"George, that's ridiculous," Laura countered. "You're talking about your managers as if they're all bad guys. They want good results as much as you do. If they knew how to get them, they'd be doing it."

"But the results are good—for them," George answered. "They make their plans for worker motivation and look heroic. They still get their BMW's and Mercedes-Benzes, because they're always tackling crises and looking like supermen. But we wouldn't have these snarl-ups in the first place if they thought things through and made changes. I'm no college graduate, but I could tell them how to improve some things overnight."

"Isn't that what I've been telling you all along?" Laura said. "But you know, you do have to be fair. Making changes isn't always that easy."

"I guess you're right. But are these guys paid huge salaries just to do easy stuff? They're just scared as hell. What if their plans went wrong? Most of them would rather stay in their offices and solve problems one of their buddies has made—or maybe one of their own. But making changes in the system? Well, that takes guts."

***

The realization that he must get out of a no-win situation finally came to George by an unexpected route. Laura was taking care of her young nephew one Saturday, and the three of them were in the local park. George sat on a metal rocket while Laura and the little boy got on the teeter-totter. Laura sang:

> *See saw, Marjorie Daw,*
> *Johnny shall have a new master.*
> *He shall have but a penny a day,*
> *Because he can't work any faster.*

The little boy laughed as they bumped up and down. Something about the words alerted George, and he repeated them to himself. "Weird song," he shouted to Laura. "What's it supposed to mean?"

"How should I know?" laughed Laura. "Nursery rhymes are just nonsense."

But it wasn't nonsense. It was a perfect description of his situation, George thought as he started to laugh. He was stuck at a ridiculously low wage because he couldn't work any faster, and it wasn't for lack of trying. The system had him locked in.

"That rhyme sure made me think," he said to Laura on the way home. "Maybe it's time for me to find a new master."

"You know what I think?" she said, giving him a penetrating look.

"What?" asked George, steeling himself for what was to come. Laura's clear-sighted common sense always sounded like wisdom to him, so it was never easy to ignore. The fact that she was a woman with no experience in manufacturing did not prevent her from seeing his situation for what it really was.

"I think you've started to sound and act like a helpless person, lately. I've seen it in your face. It's getting the same expression I've noticed on most of the guys coming out of the plant when I meet you after work: losers' faces. But you never were the type to let things get the better of you, George. So, if clearing out of the job will stop you from looking like that, I'm all for it."

Laura was delighted when he finally gave his notice. She had never considered his job or the company worthy of him. "Gutless!" she pronounced with some satisfaction. "They didn't dare do what you suggested. Didn't want to rock the boat."

"I think I'm going to rock your boat," said George, who had discovered that being pointlessly frustrated was no way to live. "I'm going to ask you to get into mine. I want you to marry me—as soon as I have another job, of course," he said with a grin.

***

George eventually found out just how close he had come to the truth at Murrow Reeves. Two managers, who were also refugees from the company, set up as rivals in the same field, and George joined them. Unknown to him at the time, they had been following a similar line of inquiry to his own. They had also calculated the loss caused by the faulty yokes and incomplete kits (with rather more precision than George had been able to) and made a formal approach to the manufacturing manager about their vendors' commitment to quality. Their well-argued case had been pushed aside.

George learned about this when he got into conversation with one of the ex-managers about his experiences at Murrow Reeves. They were both impressed by George's courage and insight, and quickly put his naturally progressive approach to good use. George learned to translate his intuitive understanding of the system into results, using statistics and charts. As he learned more about how the company worked, he realized that Murrow Reeves had been cheating itself out of tens of thousands of dollars by failing to address the problems with the materials.

That company also lost one of its most valuable resources: a person of creativity and independent thought. To them, one worker, like one faulty part, looked insignificant. But multiplied, both represented serious losses.

George, on the other hand, learned a valuable lesson from the yoke experience. He had found out a great deal about politics and about the power of inertia. He had observed the effect of a small malfunction on a large department. And he never again confused the small with the trivial.

***

LESSONS FROM THE WORKER'S STORY

Motivational Techniques Are Futile

At the beginning of the story, the manufacturing manager at Murrow Reeves gives a "Vince Lombardi" speech to try to energize the workers to do more, so that they can make their shipping numbers and improve quality. The workers are already doing as much as they can, so they are demoralized and passive. If the terminals they build fail inspection, the workers must take time to make repairs, so they fall farther behind on their quotas.

Exhortations and other kinds of incentive programs, no matter how well intentioned, cannot have the desired effect. The situation is not under the workers' control. The problems, as George's girlfriend, Laura, correctly points out, are in Murrow Reeves's system.

For Discussion:
✓   Why is Murrow Reeves's quality program, as described by the president, also a futile effort?

Problems in the System

Most people at Murrow Reeves are aware that they have a system: a set of procedures to perform repetitive tasks. Unfortunately, the system is full of informalities, flaws, and complexity. "Informalities" are the undocumented, unwritten tips and techniques that the workers use to get around problems in the system so they can do their jobs. When George talks to his supervisor, Les, and his coworker Mike, he hears about many informalities, including tips about installing the bad yoke and about hoarding spare parts in order to complete terminals on time.

There are three major flaws revealed in the story. The first is that, in order to complete the terminals, George and the other workers are forced to work around parts missing from the kits. This not only wastes time and lowers productivity, but causes more defects in the terminals. The second flaw is a bad part, which cannot perform adequately: the gray yoke. No worker can do the assembly quickly and accurately as long as he must use the gray yokes.

The third and most fundamental flaw is the set of purchasing and accounting rules, which essentially force the buyers to supply gray yokes, even though everyone knows that the more expensive white yokes can save the company a great deal of money in the long run.

For Discussion:

✓   Is purchasing at fault for the system flaws?

✓   Since people agree on what the problem is, who at Murrow Reeves should be responsible for removing the flaws?

Complexity

Complexity is a difficult concept to define, but systems containing complexity show several key symptoms. A primary symptom is the necessity of working around missing parts, equipment, resources, or information. This is the most obvious indicator of complexity at Murrow Reeves. Other symptoms are

1.   nonlinear work flow
2.   constantly making changes in the system without understanding why
3.   fractionalization (people defining a situation so that someone else is responsible for it)

For Discussion:

✓   Are any of these other symptoms of complexity present at Murrow Reeves? Where?

The Rule of Quotas, Ranking, and Numbers

Several factors in the company's structure make the problems at Murrow Reeves worse. These include the system of quotas and the system of ranking the workers. In order to make quotas and keep their jobs, the workers have to sacrifice quality, using tricks to release terminals that will likely fail when they reach customers. Since workers are ranked according to how many terminals they produce, they cannot share any helpful techniques with other workers without jeopardizing their own rankings.

This is especially ironic, given that the company makes a distinction between the new and veteran assemblers by having a two-tiered wage system. As a trainee, George feels even more intimidated about making suggestions that could help everyone meet quotas. So the entire group suffers. When George hears Laura singing the nursery rhyme, he realizes that the flaws are not with his own ability, but within the system.

Another underlying factor is the method by which the purchasing staff is judged. They must meet standard costs on the terminals' bill of materials by specifying the inexpensive but inferior gray yokes, even though this ends up costing the company millions. If the buyers try to change the parts, their jobs are in jeopardy because an accounting rule, relevant only in the short term, takes precedence over the long-term interest of the company.

The system of quotas, rankings, and incentives at Murrow Reeves does nothing but make matters worse and cause fractionalization. Workers feel isolated from each other, and different groups in the company. The workers, purchasing, and management all blame each other for the problems.

For Discussion:

✓   Where in the story can you find a constructive use of numerical evaluation?

Fear Does Damage

Employees at Murrow Reeves are justifiably concerned about their jobs and operate in an environment of fear which is counterproductive. George fears his supervisor, and the scrutiny of his coworkers, as he struggles to expose the problems. Fear causes fractionalization, which in turn causes more fear. Often, fear causes people to be passive, so that they cannot contribute as productively to the company as they are capable of doing. Through fear, Murrow Reeves ruins its most precious resource: the creativity and independent thinking of its employees.

However, George's actions are a start in the right direction. He proves that no one is helpless and no situation is hopeless. He has the guts to take the first steps toward change: refusing to accept the status quo, and asking questions. Within the limitations of his position, he tries to inform management of the need for change, and thus exercises leadership. The outcome at Murrow Reeves would have been vastly different if the management had had the fortitude—in other words, the guts—to remove the flaws from their system.

5

THE PRESIDENT'S STORY
Wealth Is More Than Money

IN THE FACULTY lounge of Wheldon College, a group of teaching staff sat together, conversing in low voices. Early afternoon sunlight sloped across the room through heavily leaded window panes, bestowing an air of venerable calm on the business-school professors as they leaned back in overstuffed armchairs.

But anyone approaching close enough to smell the upholstery leather would have seen that they were digesting more than their lunch. A piece of news received by the Dean of Studies that morning had been passed up and down the table with the bread basket, and was still the focus of intense consideration. The news was clearly not pleasing.

"I am astonished at their choice," rasped Ed Miller, a veteran professor, biting his pipe with barely concealed fury. "This man has done nothing of note for American industry. It's like awarding the Nobel Prize to a scientist who doesn't bother to use control groups or document his work properly."

"Noah Anderson has been making waves for some time," quietly observed Eric Cosell, the Dean, as if rehearsing arguments to himself. "He's still a bit of an unknown quantity, it's true. Certainly his methods are nowhere near the point where this college could endorse them. I have to admit I'm surprised that the Trustees have chosen him to give the Alumnus of the Year Lecture." He stared at the green carpet as he slowly delivered his pronouncement on the situation.

105

Miller's reply came back like a rifle crack. "The man's a nuisance. He's welcome to jeopardize his own company if he wishes. But I don't want him coming here, covered in glory, to undermine our teaching."

Boris Kaval, senior lecturer in business ethics, was still energetically pacing up and down behind the armchairs, as if he couldn't sit still. "I think you're being a little harsh, Ed. We barely know anything about the man, apart from what we've read in the press."

"You're wrong there, my friend," announced Miller, an air of prickly importance coming over him. "I know him very well. I taught him."

Looking through the mullioned glass at the lawns below, Boris felt an uprush of impatience at the die-hard attitudes of some of his colleagues. He sometimes wished that he belonged with the students crossing the grass down there, who had their futures ahead of them. At forty-five, with a long academic career already behind him, he was beginning to feel the dust of academia affecting him like a skin irritation.

"With all respect, Ed, surely a student who is considered unsatisfactory in his early twenties doesn't have to be labeled that way for the rest of his life? Anderson may have changed since then. It must be at least fifteen years since he was a student here."

"That's typical of you, Boris," said Gordon Cadwallader, who was thoroughly enjoying the controversy. "It's fortunate you didn't join the legal profession and become a judge. Nobody would ever have gotten a verdict out of you." Gordon, with his shock of bright red hair and permanent look of sardonic merriment, viewed all human activity as raw material for his observations on norms and deviations, consistencies and inconsistencies.

Gordon was the most recent arrival on the staff of Wheldon College. Its small size and intense jealousy of a well-deserved reputation made Gordon unsuitable in many ways for his post as professor in quantitative methods. This was not because of his academic ability, which was first-rate, but because of an irrepressible tendency to tease, and a total inability to keep his opinions to himself.

Eric Cosell was saying, "As far as I can remember, Noah Anderson had already worked for several years, and even run a business of sorts, when he started on the MBA program here."

"That was what made him so insufferable," muttered Ed. "Thought he knew everything. He was one of the most arrogant students I ever had the misfortune to teach."

"Arrogant or not, the guy seems to be on the right track," said Gordon. "According to an article I read recently in the *Wall Street Journal,* he bases a lot of what he does on statistics. He may be radical, but rationality is at the root of his radicalism." Gordon grinned broadly at his own play with words. His mathematician's view of the world concealed a sound knowledge of classical languages, which he played with as flamboyantly as he played with numbers.

"What none of you seems to understand," said Ed, impatience filling the air along with his pipe smoke, "is that this man's methods are completely at odds with all we consider sound practice. You're right, he is a radical and a freewheeler. He believes you can let workers on a production line manage their own jobs. I remember him saying things to that effect when he was here. He places no value on a proper management structure. He thinks anarchy and creativity are one and the same. Believe me, I know."

Boris sighed and turned back to the group. One member had not spoken. Max Hakasawa was a Japanese American who taught finance. Nobody had ever managed to break through his deep reserve, but when he expressed an opinion, everyone listened.

"Everything we've said so far is based on conjecture," Max began. "We really need to find out more about the man as he is now. I think we can do that while he's here. It'll be almost a week, isn't that right, Eric? We need to keep a closer eye on him than we usually do in these circumstances: find out what the man's really about." There was a moment of silence.

"That'll be a bit late, won't it?" said Miller, his teeth clamped around his pipe. "I'm not sure if I'm prepared to have him come at all."

Eric's pale blue eyes fluttered in consternation. "Ed, there's really not much we can do about that now. The invitation was sent a couple of days ago. We're already late in getting this event arranged. We originally invited Kurt Gamble, but the poor fellow had a heart attack shortly after he accepted."

"I'm not surprised," said Gordon, throwing back his head in an imitation of agonized collapse. Ed threw him a disapproving look. Boris groaned inwardly. The man really does behave like an eighth-grader at times, he thought.

"Let's be serious," he said. "The Trustees saw fit to invite Noah Anderson so his ideas can't be totally at odds with our own. Max is right, we'll have to take extra care about the kinds of situations he gets into. We can't stop him from saying what he wants to say. We are living in a free country, you know, Ed."

Boris paused and smiled for a moment, revealing a warmth that often got lost in his habitually grave approach to life. "But we should always be with him, ready to guide the students. They can't be expected to put his theories into perspective, after all."

"Smoke him out! That's what you really mean," said Gordon, rubbing his hands together in glee. "I like this. It's beginning to resemble a good spy story. Make sure I'm there when you pick him up from the airport. We need to make sure someone frisks him properly."

***

Noah was smiling. Standing in the middle of the noisy sheet metal production area that afternoon, he seemed to have seen a joke, although the people standing around him were looking concerned.

"I mean it," he was shouting to a man named Gary, patting him on the arm. "If you'll stop worrying about the way most people do things and try this idea, everything may fall right into place. Come and tell me tomorrow what you find out."

The supervisor, Jeff, looked concerned. "Isn't this going to waste us a lot of time, Mr. Anderson?" he said. "A lot of other people will be held up if this doesn't work out."

"It's worth trying. I'm always telling you folks that I'm

willing to accept a few failures. Not too many, mind you. But if they happen in the interest of finding out something new, I'll close my eyes to them."

Gary was a tall, muscular man in his early fifties. He was gazing at a cart piled with metal sheets for refrigerator boxes. The screw holes had been punched out by the machine next to it, and the whole pile was now due to be moved to another station. At each point, the heavy sheets were moved manually; often, he had to do it himself.

This was okay in the days when two or three sides had to be moved in each batch. But the volume of material moving through this department had grown fivefold over the past year. Gary had coped with the increases, but all of a sudden he realized he couldn't any longer. He was like a person who gradually gains weight until, suddenly one morning, his pants won't button. He was tired, cranky, and feeling his age.

He had told his supervisor, who told his manager, and they had considered hiring another man to do the job. Gary was nervous. He didn't want to be pushed aside by a younger man, even though he knew he'd be guaranteed a job somewhere else in the plant.

Noah had arrived in the department while the discussion between Gary and his supervisor was going on. He'd thought for a couple of moments and then pointed at a small overhead crane standing by the wall. "What's that used for?" he asked.

"Moving heavy machinery," replied Jeff. "It was used more in the days when we were getting equipment into this place."

"Well then, let's press it back into service," said Noah, "to help Gary."

Jeff looked doubtful. "It's old, Mr. Anderson. And it's not designed to move metal sheets. It doesn't have the finesse. For all I know, it might not even be safe."

"It can't be that old, Jeff. After all, this company only started six years ago. I know things grow obsolete fast, but this is powerful enough to do most jobs. If we talk to one of the engineers, he should find a way to adapt it." Noah started to walk away, but then looked back over his shoulder, the impish grin back on his face.

"Old machinery, old workers—well, Gary, we're not in our twenties any longer, are we. But both of us, and that old crane, still have an awful lot to give, given a good chance. Pair us all up, and you never know what sort of a powerhouse you might end up with."

Walking along the corridor to his office, Noah started thinking about a conversation he'd had some time ago with a Japanese engineer, who had told him how machinery was almost never thrown out in his company, but carefully and imaginatively adapted to new demands. Creativity of this kind was highly prized where he came from.

As the grandson of thrifty Scandinavian immigrants who settled outside Minneapolis, Noah knew that making one item serve many purposes helped create riches. As a boy, he had observed his grandparents' resourcefulness in making their possessions do multiple duty. He had taken great delight in helping his grandmother convert an old-fashioned baby carriage into a suitable whelping box for her pregnant terrier. The casing of an old wooden radio that no longer worked, ended up on the porch with nasturtiums cascading out of it. His grandfather even managed to make a passable coffee table out of the top of a dresser whose drawers had collapsed.

Later on, Noah had used his well-honed natural skills to create some of the items that every boy needs: a scooter, which was made out of a broken ironing-board and the wheels from an abandoned lawn mower, for example. Some of his inventions had a distinctly eccentric look, and he was occasionally teased by the other boys. But this did not dampen his satisfaction at what he had made.

As a man with more than enough money to spend these days, Noah was still bothered by the American habit of using money instead of brainpower to solve problems. After the initial buying of capital equipment when the company started up, he had strongly resisted further expenditure on the latest fads of automation or state-of-the-art computer equipment. He had transferred his grandparents' flair for making do into a company principle.

"Only buy a new knife when you've done everything you can

do with the one you've got," he would quip. "No robots until things are running without a hitch with the resources we have."

Some people considered him tightfisted. But few could deny that he was generous with his time, his humor, and his concern for the human beings in his employ. He was often on hand to make suggestions about getting the best out of a system, and his inventiveness was legendary.

A slight man who looked surprisingly young for the power he wielded so lightheartedly, Noah had, by his own admission, been a job-hopper. He had changed positions (always moving upward) five times in the eight years since he scraped through Wheldon, leaving a trail of stories and a bonfire of controversy behind him.

Now, as he entered his office, he was in for a surprise. His secretary could hardly contain the news: a letter from Wheldon College, his alma mater and the place where he had learned the theoretical basis of business. It was an invitation to give the Alumnus of the Year lecture. This was truly an accolade from the small but highly prestigious college.

Reading the letter, which was couched in almost as many honorifics as a communication from an oriental potentate, Noah realized he wasn't going to get much time to prepare the lecture: a mere six weeks. This gave him a strong suspicion that the Board of Trustees' first choice for Alumnus of the Year had refused the invitation for some reason.

It was hard to believe that he had been chosen after all the disagreements he'd had with the faculty, as a student. But the press had given him a lot of favorable coverage recently, and he could only assume that those old enchantresses—fame, fortune, and time—were working their magic on the old codgers at the college.

Noah made a phone call to Stewart, an engineer with a flair for finding smooth solutions to knotty problems, and asked him to have a look at the crane in Gary's division. "Stew, figure out what we can do to adapt that old overhead crane in the sheet metal division to the problem of moving refrigerator sides and doors from one station to another. The whole system of moving heavy parts seems to need consideration. It's getting too much for Gary down there, and probably for some of the others, too. These carts look antiquated; they look ripe for an accident too."

"I've been thinking of getting in there with some charts anyway, Noah," Stewart replied. "We've been so busy taking the bugs out of the welding and punching systems, that we've neglected to look at the time we're wasting on inefficient transportation of parts. It could help to speed our cycle times, if we could get it in sync with everything else."

"Great. I'm open to the idea of buying specialized equipment for this, but not until we've gotten the system as bug-free as possible. Even then, I think a bit of ingenious adaptation might get that old crane working again. Rope in Jeff and Gary. They'll have some good ideas."

After that, Noah dictated a letter to Wheldon, accepting the invitation with great pleasure.

***

Arriving at the airport in Glen Ridge, New York, Noah sniffed the aroma of tulip trees and hot earth, mixed with the fumes of aircraft fuel, and took a momentary hop back into the past.

He didn't have much time for nostalgic reflection. A young woman wearing a navy suit approached him with a nervous smile. She held out her hand. "I'm Sarah Melcher. Dr. Cosell asked me to pick you up and take you back to Wheldon." She handed him an envelope with his name written on it in a large, cultured hand. "He felt you might like time to recover from your journey before meeting them all."

Noah thanked her and followed her out to the parking lot. He dumped his suitcase in the trunk of the car and his briefcase on the back seat. "Exams coming up soon?" he asked as she started the engine.

"Not yet. Everything comes to a head next week, after the festivities are over," she replied with a rueful smile. "It's not the exams that are bothering me though. It's the prospect of an unguided landing on the world of corporate America."

Noah looked puzzled for a moment. "Unguided? But I thought it was guidance you'd been getting this past year."

"That's true, in a way. Wheldon's an excellent school, as you obviously know. But I can't help wondering how much good all our theory is really going to do when we hit reality."

"I wondered the same thing," said Noah. "And I had most of my learning to do over again."

He slit open the envelope. *Dear Noah,* the letter read, *We hope you had a good journey. I apologize for not being there to meet you, but we all look forward to meeting you this evening. We plan to meet at six o'clock in the Faculty Club for cocktails before dinner. Please join us. Yours, Eric.*

Noah wondered for a moment whether this smooth beginning would continue unhampered by conflict in the days to come. "Intentions and reality often have little to do with each other," he remarked to Sarah. "I'm hoping to get a chance to talk about that subject with you and the other students."

When Noah entered the Faculty Club, dressed in a beige cotton suit and red striped shirt, he saw before him an array of academics who resembled a gathering of junior diplomats waiting to welcome a creature from outer space. He wondered for a moment who should be more nervous: he or they.

Cosell broke away from the group and extended his thin hand. "We're glad to see you again, Noah. This is quite an occasion. Wonderful to see a student come back who has made such waves in the world."

The other staff were introduced, one by one. Miller remained in studied conversation with another professor, until he could hold out no longer. Then he shot out his hand toward Noah. The others had hoped he might muster a smile, but he was unable to bring one forth. "We've read a lot about you, Anderson. You seem to be quite notorious these days."

Noah smiled at him. "The more things change, the more they stay the same, eh? I guess boisterous students never die, they simply become boisterous in another arena, Dr. Miller. I'm glad to see you again."

***

After breakfast the next day, Boris took Noah for a walk around the grounds and gave him his itinerary. "We thought you'd like to visit some of the classrooms, get involved in some of the discussions," he said. "The students would value your input, and if they get to know you a little, your speech will be all the more meaningful."

"Yes, absolutely. I'd like that very much," concurred Noah. He was curious to know what message Wheldon was putting across these days: whether it had progressed with the times, whether the professors really knew anything about the outside world of business beyond what they saw on their consulting visits.

"I hope you don't object to my asking, but what are you proposing to speak about?" Boris inquired, trying to keep the eagerness out of his voice.

"I'm going to talk about my own company. This is not just an ego trip, but Neotech is my research laboratory. I've learned an awful lot there, and so has everyone who has worked with me. Not that I would recommend using a living company this way. But everything I say, I've lived. I personally made these ideas part of the official policy from the day the company opened."

"An enviable position to be in, though a little daunting too, I should think."

"I don't think I hesitated," said Noah. "As an employee, I experienced nothing but frustration. Everything I did was at odds with what my bosses wanted me to do. And yet I was stubbornly convinced that I was right. I tried putting into practice what I'd been taught—Taylor's principles of management, for example. But I did it atrociously because I was deeply convinced they were wrong. I got fired whichever way I played it."

Boris looked at him out of the corner of his eye. He hardly knew how to feel about such frankness. He was not accustomed to people who were so open about their less popular views, or parts of their past that didn't fit in with a nearly flawless image of themselves.

"With my track record, nobody believed I could start up a company that would last more than six months," Noah went on. "But I decided I'd do it anyway, using the principles I'd been developing at all those different companies—beginning with my teenage attempts to blow the competition in fireworks sky-high."

Boris looked puzzled for a moment. Then he remembered Miller saying how Noah thought he knew everything when he arrived. No doubt it was his fireworks business that had given him so much youthful experience.

"Tell me more about that," Boris inquired, hoping to prod Noah into more indiscreet revelations about his past.

"I found a way to make spectacular fireworks one summer when I was seventeen. In the weeks before the Fourth of July, I went into production. The demand was enormous. My prices were better than any of the stores could match, and my fireworks measured up very well. They made me rich, by my own standards at the time." They both laughed.

"I ran the company, which was called Big Bang Theory, until my final year at college. It paid for all my extracurricular expenses, although I was lucky enough to have had some financial aid from a foundation. Maybe more important was what it taught me. I did every job myself: manufacturing, managing, selling, and marketing. I even learned a bit about finance, though thankfully I didn't have a payroll to meet then.

"I did pay a few pals by the hour for their help though, whenever I could afford it. I suppose that's when I learned that exploiting your workers was out of the question. They demanded what they were worth, and I knew that their lives often depended on it—even if that only meant having enough money to impress their current lady."

"Fireworks to refrigerator panels. And you've stuck to your principles through hot and cold," Boris mused, with a trace of amusement in his voice.

"I hope I have. But most of those friends probably would have been horrified if they'd known then what I would go on to do. It wasn't fashionable in those days to make money, although people were happy enough to get it if they could. We all thought that business was mere money chasing. I discovered that there was much more involved than that: It was both more serious and more fun. Henry Ford said the same thing back in the early twenties, though I thought for a long time, in my youthful arrogance, that I was the first person to discover it."

"This sounds like the beginning of a lecture," said Boris. "Why don't you give it to the students? It's almost nine o'clock."

***

"Anybody know who said the following?" Noah was standing in the front of the classroom, not at the lectern but between two rows of students, his hand balanced lightly on a desk. *"The minutes we spend in becoming expert in finance we lose in production. The place to finance a manufacturing business is the shop, and not the bank."*

He looked around him. "Dave Packard?" ventured one of the students.

"Not a bad try," said Noah, shaking his head. "Most of what Packard has said, this guy said too. But the writer I just quoted has been in eclipse for a long time, despite his very considerable and hard-won wisdom."

"It was the original Henry Ford," said a student from the back.

"Right," agreed Noah. "Do you know what he went on to say?"

"A lot of self-righteous things about the brilliance of his own company, I believe, sir." There was scattered laughter.

Noah considered for a moment. "Well, you could say that Henry Ford was a little self-righteous. I'm sometimes the same way, so I recognize a brother in vice when I come across one. But he was passionate about his beliefs, and I think he made some good points. Let's consider."

Noah walked back to the lectern and opened Henry Ford's *My Life and Work.* He had no idea he would so enjoy being in front of a class. He had been invited in as a guest, to field a few of the students' questions for a few days. But it seemed, at least to Max Hakasawa who was busy looking at the highly polished toes of his shoes, that Anderson had all but taken over the class.

Noah started to read: *"Manufacturing is not to be confused with banking, and I think there is a tendency for too many business men to mix up in banking and for too many bankers to mix up in business. The tendency is to distort the true purposes of both business and banking, and that hurts both of them. The money has to come out of the shop, not out of the bank. I have found that the shop will answer every possible requirement, and in one case when it was believed that the company was rather seriously in need of funds, the shop raised a larger sum than any bank in this country could loan."*

A young woman in the middle of the classroom raised her hand. Noah realized it was Sarah. "Mr. Anderson, what Ford said in the twenties was very logical for his time. But the competition was negligible by comparison with today's. Ford was the only car manufacturer during that period. He could afford to be a purist."

"We can still afford to be. In fact, we can't afford not to be," countered Noah. "The more complicated life becomes, the more dedicated we have to be to what really matters. And that is not financial planning or forecasting. It is producing the best goods as efficiently as possible. The greatest companies in the world—the ones that will always be remembered for the quality of their products, their attitude, and service—these are the ones that don't make profits their primary goal. They know that if they do their job right, the profits will follow naturally. If they don't, it's usually because of a fault in their production, not in their financial planning."

A dozen hands shot up. The classroom seemed to have heated up. A student in the front row spoke out: "Are you telling us, sir, that responsible employers shouldn't look at their books? Should they ignore the financial direction of the company and jeopardize the jobs of all their employees?"

"Of course they must know where they are, financially speaking. But most people assume that if companies finance out of retained earnings, or make the shop pay for itself, they do it with gritted teeth, as a gesture to an outdated ideal. Financial planning is not just making sure the operation pays. It has become, in many companies, a huge monolith which employs the energies and minds of armies of people. These people are paid enormous sums because of the great reverence we all have for people in the financial field. But what do they do? They play with the unknown and the unknowable."

Noah paused and surveyed the field of faces in front of him. Some looked puzzled, some annoyed. Hands were still waving.

"Making financial predictions is part of the art of running a business. Companies today cannot live hand-to-mouth," protested a student.

"But that's just what they're doing," said Noah. "The financial planners can't know any more about the future than soothsayers in the Roman marketplace. Even if they base their predictions on past events, precise mathematical calculations, and other sophisticated things, there is absolutely no way we can know ahead of time most of the big factors that affect business in this country. Let's think about some of those factors."

"Trade embargoes against the Japanese," said one student.

"The Wall Street Crash," said another.

"The chip-dumping agreements, which had the opposite effect from the one intended on our electronics companies." The suggestions kept coming.

"AIDS on health insurance companies."

"Earthquakes in California."

"The greenhouse effect on heavy industry."

"Right," said Noah. "Events like these are major. But minor ones can also make nonsense of financial plans. And such unpredictable events occur all the time. In one stroke, they can undo the work of the best financial planners. These people are often at sea, yet they are heavily rewarded for skills which are contributing in an uncertain way, at best."

"So what do you suggest?" asked one young man, whose face wore an expression of sarcasm. "Let the ship toss until it hits a rock?"

"Not at all," replied Noah evenly. "You need to know your financial direction as far as it can be known, and make sure that you don't hit any obvious rocks. But something else is more important: to design the ship so that it can withstand the blows when they come. This means making your predictions in an area where you can have better control. The place you people should put your energy is where the goods are created, where the real wealth of a company resides: the production-room floor."

"Are you saying that the production area isn't subject to unpredictable events?"

"It sure is. But first, events there tend to have a less drastic effect than events the financial world is heir to. Second, they can be surprisingly well controlled if we will give up some of our old ideas of the meaning of control."

"Could you give some concrete examples, Mr. Anderson?"

"Let me talk about my own company, because that's what I know best. In fact, it may be all I really know. I've never been good at theory, and I've come by most of my learning in a very pragmatic way.

"I'll tell you first that we do almost nothing to control our workers' productivity. They are already doing their best without being goaded. What we all try to control is the process itself. I train my workers to watch and question all the time how we might improve processes: cut down waste, rework, scrap, unnecessary maneuvers, wasted floor space. Suggestions are part of the daily diet in my company. Some don't work, but we always look at them. When we do try something out, we chart it, to see what difference it's making. So we know whether to carry on or try something different. It's a game and most people love it."

Another student interjected, "I read that you're rather reluctant to spend money on new technology. Didn't *Forbes* magazine say you'd run into trouble some day because of being so tightfisted?"

Noah smiled ruefully. "Well, I'm from Scandinavian stock, but I do act like a Scot sometimes. I'm very mean about spending capital sums on new technology until I'm sure it is absolutely necessary. A lot of people think technology is the great panacea. But it should never be installed in a company without spring cleaning first. That means ironing out all the wrinkles in your manufacturing process and getting rid of all unnecessary complexity.

"If you get rid of complexity, you often find the manufacturing process becomes so efficient that not as much automation is necessary. But if you automate without first getting rid of complexity, you cast complexity in concrete. And that could strangle your whole manufacturing system."

"But surely, it's the president who has to take the company into the future; to look at new ways of doing things," queried a student. "Aren't automation and imaginative use of the financial system a part of that future?"

"Not at the expense of people or efficiency," Noah replied. "As CEO, I see my role primarily as a manufacturer. If there are problems in the company, we don't borrow money. We solve the problems. We increase our material turns, reduce our cycle times, find ways to reduce defect rates more, and then still more. We do it by detecting places where our process isn't as good as it could be. The exhilarating thing is that there's no end to the improvements we can make. However good we are, we can always get better. It takes ingenuity, I can tell you. But that's where minds like yours come in."

Noah looked toward Sarah, and smiled. "You're probably right about self-righteousness. Henry Ford and I do have that in common. We both boast shamelessly about our companies."

Hakasawa held up his hand and pointed at the large clock on the wall. "I think most of the students have other classes or appointments to go to at eleven-thirty. I hope you'll all forgive me if I ask Mr. Anderson to bring his talk to an end. Thank you, Mr. Anderson. What you said was most interesting and informative."

There was a second of silence before the students started to applaud. Hakasawa looked bemused as he joined the applause. They stood for several moments, clapping, before filing out, for a moment liberated from the book-learning that weighed them down.

As they walked down the steps from the classroom to the quad, Boris appeared on the bottom step and started walking up to meet them. The group came to a halt between flourishing displays of orange and blue flowers that bordered the steps.

"The students are buzzing even louder than the bees around here," Boris remarked. "What kind of nectar have they been sipping?"

Noah smiled. He instinctively liked Boris, despite his slight pomposity. "I took up far too much of Max's class time," said Noah, apologetically.

"That's what we hoped you'd do," Max replied evenly. "You got them well stirred up. We've covered many of the alternate theories of financing, from the most conservative to the most modern. But you've given them some hard questions to ask about what they've learned."

Noah looked at him sideways, a quizzical expression on his face. "Mr. Hakasawa, I hope you won't be offended if I say what I really think. The heavy emphasis on financial planning and forecasting in most management courses—and that includes Wheldon's—is misleading for the students. What they see is that society values and pays the people who can play with numbers. So this is the field that steals the most ambitious, and sometimes the best students away from the real areas of challenge."

"But finance is enormously challenging," replied Max, with pride. "It probably does attract the best minds, for that reason. You may not feel it's useful, but all of American business is based on it. I don't think you can deny that."

"Based on it partly because the social order that prevails in our corporations has decreed that it should be this way?" Noah said. His eyebrows asked a question, but his eyes stated a fact.

Noah started walking down the steps again and Boris fell in line. Students were already grouped at the bottom of the steps, waiting. Some were starting up toward Noah, challenge in their faces, questions in their eyes.

"Mr. Anderson, please explain what you mean when you say that financial forecasting is no better than soothsaying. Isn't that what you said?" Sarah was asking the question, her eyes blazing.

"Is there anywhere we can be more comfortable?" asked Noah. "I'd like to talk but I can't resist these campus lawns. I want to enjoy them to the hilt while I'm here. Much more inviting than the floor of a sheet metal shop."

"I'll stay," said Boris in an undertone to Max.

The students drifted to an area on the other side of the lawn, where the rim of the fountain provided a good seating area and some wooden benches provided extra audience room.

Noah waited until everyone looked comfortable, then he repeated, "It's true. We're not much better than the Romans when it comes to putting our faith in the people with the ability to pull the wool over our eyes. I will try to explain why. As I see it, financial forecasting is based on assumptions similar to the ones nineteenth-century physicists held about the nature of matter. They thought physical properties were stable and predictable. But as it turned out, they weren't. In the same way, financial theory pretends that predictions are possible: that factors are stable and will not turn head-over-heels on us at any given moment, or metamorphose into something else."

"But the financial people at our companies seem to be doing all right," objected one student. "They do their jobs, they live well, their companies are growing in many cases. Why should we be idealistic and go for jobs that pay less?"

"You may be in for a shock," said Noah. "Up to now, we have all been cushioned by the system. Companies pay big money to the people who play with the figures. But it may not go on much longer. Too many of our companies are living on borrowed money and borrowed time. If real wealth doesn't catch up with the figures, we'll all be in the soup."

"I agree," chimed in another student. "By letting a top-heavy financial system rule our companies, we're taking our companies further and further into debt and uncertainty—just like the nation itself—and finding ways to justify it."

"So what about wealth? How do we get it—either for our companies or ourselves?" came a question from the fountain.

"There are ways to create tremendous wealth; real wealth, as opposed to mere money. It's by getting back to reality on the factory floor. We have to start looking at that. Then, we can start moving into the future."

***

That evening, a reporter from the local paper arrived on campus. By the time she had progressed to Noah himself, she had already taped several conversations, and was ready with some biting questions.

"Mr. Anderson, you seem to have a reputation as a rebel. I hear you're putting forward a lot of ideas that are not the accepted line of thought here. Are you attacking the philosophy of your own school?" Sally Casement's voice was brittle as she thrust the microphone toward his mouth.

"Absolutely not. I am trying to tell the students, and anyone else who wishes to listen, what I believe to be the right way to proceed."

"And what is the truth, as you see it?"

"I didn't use that word, please note. There may be more to truth than can be told in a paragraph or two and then edited down to a pithy headline in your newspaper." Noah looked out toward the line of trees that edged the lawn, now blazing with the evening sun as it sank behind them.

"But let me put it like this," he went on. "I believe in not overcomplicating things, and in taking the most direct route available to your goal. That means creating wealth with the means at your disposal: your hands, brain, and the minimum of materials necessary. Translated into today's industrial scene, that means designing a manufacturing system as free of complexity as possible.

"When you remove complexity, fewer things can go wrong, and people work to get optimal use out of each piece of equipment. Often, because they use their ingenuity, they find that expenditure on new equipment is not necessary. If we look carefully at a problem in a production line, we find it's not due to lazy or careless workers but to the way things are set up: Often, small details are complexities that do nothing but give opportunities for error and are a waste of time and energy. The effect of removing them is sometimes surprising."

"Describe some of the effects," demanded the reporter, who now had a glazed expression on her face.

"In the case of my own company, let's see . . . We reduced our defect rates from a not-too-bad ten to fifteen percent to less than one percent. Our cycle times are always being improved. It's a continuous process, so sometimes it's hard to know what to compare it to. But I can only tell you that it takes us twenty-four hours to produce what one of our competitors does in twenty-four days. We've reduced our standard costs by a factor of three in the past year, without automation. And our machine uptime is outstanding—about ninety-four percent, which is far above the industry average. In every case, we made the improvements by reducing complexity. It's as simple as that."

"And what about the financial aspects? I'm told you were contradicting most of what the students here have been taught. They're upset. They have exams next week, and they're confused."

Noah laughed. "Poor kids! A contradiction—how terrible! I don't think challenges of this sort are unheard of in the business world. People may complain that the schools are churning out MBA's faster than the best production lines they learn about. But a little intellectual pain still gets into the works from time to time, maybe even helps oil it."

By the time the reporter had finished with him, it was past time for dinner. No doubt, the faculty members having their pre-dinner drink in the senior common room would have aired the subject of his class discussions thoroughly. Noah wondered what the atmosphere would be like at dinner.

Walking in late, he saw that Boris had kept the chair next to him empty. Most of the rest of the faculty had already eaten and departed. Noah realized suddenly how exhausted he was, and sank into the ladder-back chair, grateful at the prospect of food.

As he started on his leek and potato soup, he realized his throat was sore. "I don't think I have much voice for conversation, Boris. I've hardly stopped talking all day."

"You certainly have fielded a lot of questions. Would you like to take a few moments by yourself? We could meet for coffee in the common room."

As he sat eating his fish in the deserted dining room, Noah suddenly became aware of the silent judgmental gazes of a dozen past deans of Wheldon, whose likenesses adorned the gray walls. As a jury, they did not look as if they would lean towards mercy. Noah felt like a son who had quarreled with his father, been forgiven for his rebellious ways, and been invited home at last. But then, within minutes of arriving, and despite every good intention on both sides, they had started to quarrel again.

Looking up from his reverie, Noah suddenly saw Miller standing before him, on the opposite side of the table.

"Anderson," he said gruffly. "Sorry if I startled you. I must talk to you."

Noah got up, leaving his half-finished lemon mousse to the mercies of the kitchen staff. "Shall we walk outside?" Noah asked. "I'd like a little fresh air. Feeling a bit bushed, all of a sudden."

As they walked along the gravel path that bordered the front of the imposing gray stone building, Miller's head was bent, his hands clasped behind him. "Anderson, you've achieved notoriety, even fame. Your company is doing well, and I congratulate you. But your methods are unorthodox. They may work for you, but they cannot be imposed on our students at whim, especially just before their examinations."

"Dr. Miller, I don't think I've imposed anything. I've merely raised questions. These students are going to be influential, each one affecting the lives of hundreds of people. It's important they know more than theory. The world out there is complicated, and changing all the time."

Miller's face turned a shade brighter in the dim light from the windows. He stopped, pulled his pipe and tobacco out of his baggy jacket pocket, and started to fill it from the pouch.

"I suppose you think we're not aware of all that?" he said, a sarcastic edge to his voice.

"I don't think it's possible to be completely aware unless you're bearing the brunt of some of the changes, or the threat of change. The underpinnings of business strategy, that is, the theory, is very important. Your students are getting it here. They're bright, knowledgeable, argumentative. But they don't have much of an idea of how they'd go into a company and increase its output of, say, buttons or hubcaps or cathode ray tubes."

"We're teaching them how to manage, not how to manipulate a production area," Miller shot back. "These students are not aiming to be engineers or manufacturing managers."

"But what I'm contending is that they've got to stop thinking they're above all that. We all have to stop boxing people into hierarchies which compartmentalize their knowledge and set one faction against another. Managers need to communicate with engineers, they need to understand technology, they need firsthand experience of production. If they put their considerable brainpower to work on what is going on in all these areas, we might see an enormous surge of productivity in this country."

"I admire your idealism, Noah. But you've always been inclined to get a little carried away by ideas. You haven't changed much in that respect." He tried to muster a smile.

"But it's not idealism." Noah suddenly remembered vividly how exasperated he used to get in class arguments with Miller. This was almost like a replay, right down to the smell of tobacco. "It's very real. I seem to be blowing my trumpet a lot at the moment, but you know Neotech's growth has exceeded all expectations. And it's not because of number manipulation. It's not at the expense of our workers either."

Noah decided, at risk of irritating Miller further, to abandon modesty and spell out some of the achievements that gave him the most personal satisfaction. People were always talking about Neotech's runaway success, but few seemed really to understand how or why it was doing so well.

"We have the lowest employee turnover I know of. People actually come up and tell me how glad they are to be working for us. I may be tight with capital expenditure, because I don't rush for the latest technology until I've seen how we can do better on our own. But I'm not tight with wages and benefits. My people are rewarded for what they do well, regardless of their position in the company."

"A sort of capitalist socialism," said Miller, a scathing note in his voice.

"I hate labels," said Noah. "They destroy people's perceptions of what's really going on. There's no charity, if that's what you mean. Each person's contribution, at whatever level, is really vital and everyone knows that. So people in the so-called lowly jobs give far more of their inventiveness, skill, and knowledge than most managers ever realize they have."

"So what about your bottom line?" asked Miller. "Don't you control your finances?"

"We make a point of controlling them, and everything else," said Noah, for the first time that day finding it hard to control his own irritation. "That's why we don't like to rely on financing from outsiders—which is often the beginning of the end of real control for a company. If things go wrong with our finances, we look to see what's amiss elsewhere. We go back to the manufacturing line and yes, the financial people get in there too.

"The people who calculate the profit margins are the ones who usually drive the ritziest cars. But to me, that position is hardly more important than that of the gilded lady at the prow of a sixteenth-century galleon. She looks pretty and impressive, but she's there more for show than results. She may give the ship pride in herself, like the financial officers' Mercedes-Benzes and BMW's parked out in front. But the ship itself is what's important: the rudder, hull, sails, and the crew. That's where I focus my own efforts and the efforts of my best people."

"So if you're not looking at superstitious images like profit margins to gauge the success of your company, where are you looking?" asked Miller, puffing hard.

"I rate the success of my company in terms of our workers' security and standard of living, rather than the balance sheet. My people are rewarded for what they do well, regardless of their position in the hierarchy. Of course, there are differences in salary and wage scales, but they are not as gross as the usual ones I hear of."

"I'm sure you have no trouble in finding loyal workers," said Miller. "But how do you attract good executives at salaries that can't be that high?"

"Who says they're not?" asked Noah, a boyish glint in his eye. "Neotech's doing well, you know. But you're right, some of my competitors do offer higher salaries to their executives. But mine get other things. Security. Profit-sharing. More time to spend with their families and pursue other things they think are important. I don't go for the idea that a man has to sell his soul to his company."

A couple of students strolled along the path in their direction, and greeted them as they passed. They were deep in conversation about a hypothetical situation they would have to solve. It was a classic question in business school and Noah picked it up immediately. He realized how much students need the freedom to throw ideas around and how quickly that freedom evaporates once they start treading the tightrope of corporate career paths.

"The other thing we have at Neotech," he went on after a pause, "is a situation where people can take risks without fear of a backlash. In our philosophy, we assume people do their best. We try to help them make improvements in the system so that their best won't be snarled in some obstacle somewhere. We've also scrapped annual reviews and inquisitional tools that serve to develop egotism and paranoia."

"Sounds like the manifesto of some newfangled political party," muttered Miller.

"Well, in some senses you're right. It does represent a change in the social order," replied Noah. "But on the other hand, it's not that complicated. We make the system self-sufficient by constantly refining and improving it. Then we try to leave it to human ingenuity to come up with ideas, solve problems, think of new and better directions at all levels. Most of the time, it really does work."

"Certainly sounds ideal," said Miller, his voice sounding almost conciliatory. "And what do you get out of all this?"

Noah looked at him. They had turned to walk back down the path, and Miller's heavily lined face was now lit by the tall open windows. Noah wasn't sure what kind of question this was, but he thought he detected a softer, more forgiving expression.

"Having ten times more money wouldn't make my life any more comfortable," he said. "I'm a happy man."

***

Back in the common room, Noah found Boris sitting by himself near an imposing cabinet full of antique porcelain jugs. Noah pulled up an armchair next to him, after balancing his coffee cup uncertainly on a small round table with three flimsy legs.

He was aware that Boris had been waiting to speak to him alone, and he was fairly sure he was in for more raps on the knuckles. Even so, he felt better about this interview than the two he had just endured with the journalist and Miller. A lecture from Boris, by comparison, seemed an almost relaxing prospect: suitable as light after-dinner entertainment by the standards of this challenging institution.

"It seems you've already had quite an effect on some of our students," Boris observed, giving a stir to his sugarless coffee. He felt suddenly both pedantic and treacherous, realizing that he was about to cross-examine a man he liked and admired. And this for the sake of loyalty to a department about which he was feeling increasingly critical. He could hear the fusty academic ring in his own voice, developed over years of exposure to meticulous common-room discussions that would sometimes bog down in tiny details for weeks.

"I hope it's been positive. I've told them what I know," replied Noah. "Everything I say comes out of my own experience, or my own observations. Not very sound, really. None of it is backed by research." He laughed and picked up the small blue-willow pattern coffee cup.

"The main thing is to get our students thinking about things," replied Boris. "Keeping their minds open is one of my jobs." Looking at the lustrous mullioned windows, now keeping the glossy spring night at bay, he wondered why nobody ever opened them. The industrialist sitting beside him seemed like a brisk breeze that had entered the room by another route. "Your comments today have probably cranked open more minds than we've managed to stimulate all year. Coming straight from the battlefield is no bad thing," he added, trying to soften his own comment.

"Yes, but you have all studied strategy more than I have. All I can give the students are details of the action out there. A bit of Indiana Jones in the workplace."

Boris hesitated and then plunged in. "Noah, I ought to tell you that some of the staff have taken your statements as a direct attack on their teaching and philosophy."

Noah's jaw jutted forward almost imperceptibly, as it always did when he was trying to control his anger, laughter, sadness, or irritation. Tonight, it was an almost equal mix of all four, with a splash of exhaustion thrown in.

"I know," he replied. "Miller confronted me in the dining room. I've just been talking to him."

Boris felt outraged. Earlier in the evening, several members of the staff had met and determined that Boris should do the dirty work of warning Noah off their territory. He was reluctant, but felt that his natural sympathy for Noah might make him the most suitable candidate. He could at least explain the situation without rancor. Now, it seemed, Miller had jumped in and done it his own way.

"Did he tell you that you were being considered for a place on the Board of Trustees?" asked Boris, playing his trump card.

Noah looked up, astonishment burning in his blue eyes. "No," he said abruptly. "Where did you hear that?"

"Gordon Cadwallader got wind of it a couple of days ago; from Eric Cosell, actually. He wasn't supposed to pass it on, but Gordon has a way of ignoring the spoken and unspoken rules of the game."

Noah rubbed his forehead hard. The Alumnus of the Year speech was one thing, the Board of Trustees quite another. This surely meant a total vote of confidence. In which case, the clear hostility from so many of the staff boded conflict ahead. Today's encounters were only skirmishes before the big battle.

"Some of the staff, Miller among them, have been to Dwight Gerber, the Chairman of the Board, and asked him to reconsider, in light of the last few days. It's a rotten business." Boris felt his breathing coming in constricted bursts, as if his lungs had iron bands around them.

"Well," Noah said, "their decision, whatever it is, won't alter anything for me. A place on the Board would be pleasant. But ultimately, it's Neotech that matters."

"I think it partially depends on what you have to say in your speech," continued Boris. "They clearly approve of who you are and the way you run your business. I suppose the final verdict will be cast on what points you emphasize."

Noah raised his eyebrows. "That sounds a bit two-faced,

Boris, especially coming from someone who teaches ethics," he said.

Boris registered shock for a moment. He realized his hands were sweating. "Obviously nobody expects you to compromise your beliefs," he said, an edge to his voice. "But there are some areas where your beliefs come into clear conflict with the curriculum of the college. You can soft-pedal those, I suppose."

"I can only tell it the way I perceive it. The areas where my ideas come into conflict with what I see being taught here are exactly the ones I need to address. It's not pigheadedness. I'm not even much of an evangelist by nature. But I can't see students being turned out of this school with what I know to be a lot of outdated ideas."

"But once on the Board, you'll have all the influence you need," said Boris. "I want you there. I think your presence would be healthy for all of us. I, for one, feel as if I could do with a shot of new attitudes," he added in an undertone.

"But what I see is scorching me now," protested Noah. "The same way it did while I was a student, though I didn't really understand why in those days. Instinctively, I fought against the elitism, the assumption of superiority by those who mastered the abstract skills such as finance and law. Now I know why. They are necessary and important skills, certainly, and our students must know them. But when they're overemphasized, they develop a life of their own, like parasites. They're sucking the blood from our nation's industrial intellect and energy. Boris, we can't afford that kind of playing around any more. Wheldon is years out of date."

Boris looked crushed. He had compromised himself to put the college's point of view to Noah; listened to gossip and spilled the beans about the Trustees' deliberations; then asked Noah to compromise his own position for the sake of self-interest, both his own and Noah's. Now he found himself listening to Noah and being swayed far too easily by his argument.

Boris took off his glasses and rubbed them with a handkerchief, a disconsolate expression on his patrician face. "Noah, I'm embarrassed to say that your points are just too big for me to discuss with you at the moment. I feel a bit worn out. Will you excuse me if I say goodnight? I'd like to continue the discussion in the morning."

"Couldn't agree more," said Noah, with some relief. He felt as if his mind was powered by a separate engine from his body, and his body was definitely running on empty. "I'm pretty tired myself."

They both got up and walked wearily out of the senior common room. Only three people were left—two talking at the other end, and the third reading a battered *Wall Street Journal* near the door. She bid them goodnight, glancing as she did at the clock on the wall. It was eleven thirty-five.

***

Down in the faculty dining room, the *Glen Ridge Observer* sat conspicuously on the breakfast table. A number of people got up and cleared out as Noah took his seat. Gordon Cadwallader, who was still wolfing down his fried eggs and Canadian bacon, waved his fork towards the paper. To Noah it had the look of an unexploded mine, sitting between the neatly curled butter pats and the wooden salt and pepper set.

"Have a look on page three. That lady was up to no good." Gordon did not look overly upset about whatever was no good, and took a large bite of toast.

Noah poured himself some coffee, opened the paper and read: *Trouble is brewing at Wheldon College between the faculty and Mr. Noah Anderson, the speaker chosen to give the Alumnus of the Year address this Saturday, May 3. A member of the class of '67, Mr. Noah Anderson is a guest for five days at the prestigious graduate school that awards 155 highly sought-after MBA's every year.*

As founder and president of Neotech, a sheet metal manufacturing company which has grown to $300 million in only six years, Anderson's reputation has grown as fast as his company. However, his approach to manufacturing and finance, is causing some dissent among staff and students. Many consider his ideas contradictory to much of the curriculum taught at the business school.

One of this year's students, who declined to be named, said he believed many of the faculty were deeply upset by Mr. Anderson's stated approach to running a business, and believed it ridiculed what was being taught at the school. There was speculation on campus as to whether Anderson's speech, planned for this Saturday, will be cancelled. An unnamed source stated that a planned invitation to Anderson to become a member of the Board of Trustees may also be withdrawn.

Noah looked toward Gordon, who was soaking up the last traces of yolk from his plate with a crust of brown toast. He was smiling, as always. "Shades of the past? I hear you had a healthy reputation as someone who could create a ruckus while you were a student here."

Noah sighed. He was not finding all this as amusing as Cadwallader apparently was. What had been intended as honest answers to questions had somehow been transformed into a writhing nest of intrigue, unpleasantness, and misunderstanding.

"I see I've already almost been offered a place on the Board of Trustees and almost had the offer withdrawn again. Fascinating. Did Sally Casement interview you?" he inquired, looking hard at Cadwallader.

"I saw her for about three minutes," Gordon replied, looking suddenly defensive. "Not time for any kind of an interview."

"But enough time to tell her your little bit of news about the Trustees and warn her to keep the quote anonymous?"

"Look, I told her no more than is general knowledge. Things get around fast in any school. I'm sure what I said was told to her by half a dozen other people too. That's probably why she went off so fast. She didn't think I had much to offer."

Noah got up, leaving his coffee virtually untouched but bundling the *Glen Ridge Observer* under his arm. He made for Cosell's office, where he found Eric peering heavily at a thin pile of papers on his desk.

"Eric, I need to be enlightened. Rumors of all kinds are coming at me. But I don't necessarily recognize them. What's this about the Board of Trustees?"

Eric looked up and slowly took off his spectacles. "What is this about the Board of Trustees? What have you heard?"

"I was going to be invited to join, but the offer is now about to be withdrawn before it gets to me; by courtesy of sources known only to Miss Sally Casement of the *Glen Ridge Observer.*" Noah put the paper, folded to frame the article, down on Eric's desk. Eric put his spectacles on again and proceeded to read the piece.

"Damn," he said finally with almost majestic deliberation. "Excuse my language but this was not what we had in mind."

"What did you have in mind?" asked Noah. "I really would like to know."

"I would have preferred to tell you this in better circumstances, but the Trustees will almost certainly offer you a place on the Board. There's no question about your qualifications for such a position. This fracas with the students and some of the staff is just the painful adjustment to new ideas. But we educators need to take a lead in the field of new ideas. They'll get over it, just as I have."

"They'll have to," countered Noah. "It's the future we're talking about."

***

Noah's wife, Ellen, flew in from Minnesota on Friday, and gave him a little coaching on his speech. "It's a good thing I came for those extra days," he told her as they walked about Wheldon's lush grounds. "I never realized how little things have changed. The big shifts in attitude need to start here, in the business schools. This one's still operating from premises that are years out of date, and I doubt if it's that unusual. My ideas represented quite a threat to some of the staff."

"They came around, then?"

"I don't quite know what happened. In the past twenty-four hours, the mood has started to turn. Even the Dean seems to have come down on my side. It may be partly because of the students' reaction. They can't get enough of reality. We've been having lively discussions that have ranged far beyond business, yet everything we've talked about is relevant."

"What about that awful newspaper article?" asked Ellen. "What got into that journalist?"

"At first, I was confused by her hostility, too. But she was right, in a way, to grill me. She needed to understand the discrepancy between all the recent articles about Neotech, and the attitude of most of the school—which was anger at that point. People usually get angry when they have to face change. It was probably a healthy reaction."

"Everyone seems very friendly now," Ellen murmured. "They've been delightful to me. Even that old Dr. Miller, who you warned me about, was quite charming."

Noah laughed. "Well, we had our disagreements this time, too. I think he felt threatened and confused. He was no longer sure what to teach, and his reaction came across as hostility. It reminded me of Thomas Jefferson when he was told a meteor had hit New England. He preferred to believe the scientists were lying than face the consequences of what they told him. But I think most people realize now that I'm not trying to be destructive. I just want to open the doors to some breezes that feel a little chilling to start with."

"Reality?" Ellen asked, smiling. She took him by the arm as they strolled past tulip trees. "Well, you've certainly had a vote of confidence. A trustee, on top of the other honors!"

"By the skin of my teeth," Noah said, baring his own teeth playfully as he looked over at her. "You'll never know how close a call that was!"

Standing on the podium that Saturday before an audience of some five hundred, Noah looked like a person with a mission to the future. He could have been an astronaut except that he wasn't wearing a silver space suit.

He talked of many things. He told them about Neotech until they felt they had been there, standing in the shoes of some of his managers, his financial officers, and his production line workers. He gave them problems to solve on the spot. He provided glimpses of new ways to tackle old problems, and old ways to solve new ones. He tickled their consciences and made them laugh. He showed them where they stood, and where they might go.

"And now comes the heavy part," he announced with a smile. "The windup. The conclusion. This is the bit where I lecture you." Even Sally Casement, sitting to the side with a much larger tape recorder and a cameraman, looked engrossed.

"Here we are, a nation that is in serious debt, underproducing and overconsuming. Everyone wants to be in the top-paying jobs—finance and law—especially you people with expensive training and excellent brainpower. Of course you want to be there. That's where the fun is, and after all your hard work, you want to get some of the action.

"I have a hunch that it's time for a little idealism to come back into our lives. We've been intent on the pursuit of money for the past decade and a half. We've been seeking personal money, which often causes rifts instead of happiness. The pursuit of wealth will be the challenge for the foremost minds of the future: the wealth of nations, to use that famous phrase coined by Adam Smith, not just of individuals.

"We are facing a change in the social order, one that no longer elevates the abstract skills at the expense of the productive ones. One that brings the best minds back to tackle the big problems. And one that brings everyone's mind back into play instead of valuing only those ideas that come from the people with the largest salaries.

"Before we go making changes, we have to thoroughly understand the system. Understanding cannot be based on opinion alone, however well informed that opinion is. We have to take data on everything that can stand improvement, and that usually means just about everything. That's a job for everyone; a cooperative detective effort, if you like, by workers and managers alike. The workers pick up the clues, and the managers must understand them before making decisions. This is the kind of leadership by cooperation we encourage at Neotech.

"The more we improve the system by removing flaws, the more time and energy all our people have to use their ingenuity, their observations, their creativity: in other words, to have fun. Everyone has a hand in improving things, in thinking of ways to tackle problems, especially the people who are down there working on those problems themselves.

"The result is that most of them feel like human beings instead of cogs in a machine. This creates wealth in every sense: a more satisfying life, as well as a better standard of living for more people.

"What we try to do is design a system that balances flexibility and predictability. To calculate everything we do down to a fraction of an inch, and still to roll with the punches, takes all the brilliance of everyone we have in the company. And that means all our people are doing what they do best—being humans—which is being more ingenious and more inventive by far than any computer ever created or likely to be created."

As Noah stepped down from the podium, he was surprised to hear applause coming at him in joyful waves, like breakers on a beach.

Faces all around seemed to be beaming; even the Dean's. As he joined the crowd on the floor of the huge assembly hall, several students came up to congratulate him and meet Ellen. Sarah gave him an unexpected, though rather shy, hug.

"This week has changed me more than all the rest of my time here," she said. "The school gave me learning, but what you've told us is more like liberation. You've given me a sense of purpose I never had before. Do you have any positions available at Neotech?"

Noah smiled as he shook his head. "It's the other companies that need you. You can visit us at Neotech and see with your own eyes what I mean. Then take what you learn with you."

"Difficult," said a student standing next to her, a smile shining through the doubt on his face.

"Difficult indeed," said Noah. "But that's the big challenge for all of us."

***

LESSONS FROM THE PRESIDENT'S STORY

The New Meaning of Wealth

Noah Anderson represents a contrast in style and substance to the academics at Wheldon College. Wheldon teaches management theories popularized in the early 1900's, which stress the development of "optimal" plans. These views are not bad, but are simply inadequate for today's business challenges. Noah views business and the underlying theories differently.

Pragmatism Works Better Than Planning

At his company, Noah interacts informally with the workers, paying attention to immediate problems (for example, how to move heavy metal sheets), and suggesting solutions. He understands that action needs to be taken to solve problems and perhaps uncover new opportunities. In Professor Hakasawa's class, Noah debunks the idea that planners, particularly financial planners, can really steer a company toward success.

Many factors that influence any system are unknown and unknowable. Therefore, no matter how good the data and the theories are, there will be surprises, and planners can be no more effective than soothsayers. The "brute force" of armies of planners is a waste of a company's resources.

While trying to make predictions is fine, Noah suggests that more attention be paid to activities that can be better controlled: those on the production floor. There will always be randomness and unexpected events. Resources expended on developing and analyzing a system will make that system more resilient to the inevitable changes and surprises.

For Discussion:

✓   Give five examples of external events that have occurred within the last year that could undermine your company's financial and business plans.

✓   What constructive actions could be taken if your company had a resilient system in place?

Technology Isn't Always the Answer

Noah hesitates to rely on the latest technology for answers to any problems at Neotech. He is neither technophobic nor cheap. Rather, as he learned from "recycling" items as a boy, putting the brainpower of his people to work toward solving problems usually works better than additional technology or money. Noah looks to, and invests in, people first. In order to be beneficial, technology should not be used as a substitute for people or efficiency.

Also, problems often indicate that there is complexity in a company's system. At Neotech, people work on removing complexity and getting optimal use out of existing equipment. Noah outlines to the reporter how defect rates went down, cycle times got shorter, and costs decreased, all without increased automation. Excess complexity should be removed before automation or new technology is tried; otherwise, complexity may be cast in concrete. Automating complexity is never as effective as removing it.

For Discussion:

✓   What solutions does Noah seek at Neotech instead of new technology?

✓   How does he make the best use of the company's existing technology?

✓   What other options does he have?

✓   What do you think the results would be?

Too Much Emphasis on Finance

In his lectures and speeches at Wheldon, plus in describing how he runs his own company, Noah points out several misconceptions about the importance of the financial functions in American business. Capital expenditure or capital borrowing should not be the initial approach to solving problems or "growing" a company, according to Noah. Financing can give a false sense of security because overcapitalization negatively affects margins and dilutes earnings.

Overemphasis on money means that financial people, often outsiders, can dictate a direction that is not in the company's long-term best interests. Why is there so much emphasis on finance in American business? Our corporate structures have arbitrarily made financial positions into glamorous, high-paying jobs, so people will naturally be attracted to them. Wheldon and other business schools reinforce this idea. Students are often told that finance is "where the action is," and manufacturing and production are often characterized as second-class careers.

A company's financial problems are nearly always symptomatic of other problems, and financial controls do not translate into manufacturing controls. Too often today, financial results can be manipulated for short-term purposes, or for show. Noah contends that standard financial measures do not reflect how well a company is really doing. He prefers to measure Neotech's success in terms of the workers' standard of living rather than the balance sheet. He sees "wealth" very differently from the others at Wheldon.

For Discussion:

✓   Is finance really the most intellectually challenging discipline at Wheldon? Why or why not?

✓   What else should business-school graduates know?

The Money Trap

In "going back to the basics," and paying attention to production, Noah has come to understand that wealth and a good-looking balance sheet are not the same. As he tells the reporter, a functioning system that produces goods or services is the source of real wealth. A company creates wealth if it makes good-quality products, with features and prices that are attractive to the marketplace, and if these products can provide respectable internal margins. This allows the company to operate as well as provide a good standard of living for its employees.

When Wheldon students and faculty accuse Noah of being idealistic or radical, he acknowledges that he must be a purist, in the sense that he needs certain theories and models to keep him on course and help him deal with intangibles. This explains his use of statistics for finding flaws in the system, his never-ending determination to remove complexity, and his focus on people as his most valuable resource.

> ### For Discussion:
> ✓　　How does removing complexity generate wealth?

People as Contributors

One of the greatest differences between Noah and the Wheldon faculty is how they approach people and the skills they offer. Jobs can be classified as using various combinations of judgment, knowledge, skill, and experience. All of these attributes, used to the fullest in every job, are essential to a company if it is to be competitive. The problem is that Wheldon and other business schools train managers in the abstract attributes of judgment and knowledge, and often actively denigrate any other jobs (even in management) that involve "doing."

In his fireworks business, Noah learned that it does not pay to exploit people, but today's business-school graduates may not learn this lesson. When these new managers run businesses, they separate themselves from other workers, and fractionalization easily occurs. By being isolated from the "shop floor," managers do not have the information needed to make the best decisions, and often do not allow people at all levels to contribute to the fullest.

To Professor Miller's consternation, Noah questions the salary structures of most companies. Is there really a justification for paying a judgment worker more than fifty times the salary of a skilled worker? At Neotech, where complexity has been reduced, less management is needed, and pay levels do not fluctuate wildly with job levels. People at Neotech get satisfaction by earning reasonable salaries and contributing freely.

Providing a good system, and encouraging people to improve it, is management's challenge. This makes sense because having people struggle to succeed in spite of the system will not be as effective as improving the system. Noah understands that the new attitude toward people does mean changes in the social order and will create resistance, but that to be at their most productive, employees must trust management and the system.

Professor Miller looks upon this attitude as a "manifesto of some newfangled political party, or capitalist socialism," but Noah is quick to emphasize that it is not charity, and it is not a soapbox agenda. It is Noah's strategy for success, and it can be America's, too.

For Discussion:

✓   Why are the faculty at Wheldon so offended by Noah's attitude toward employees?

✓   What does this say about Wheldon's "system"?

6

THE CONSULTANT'S STORY
Paradigms of Leadership

"YOU WANT TO DO a series on what? Can you speak up? I can hardly hear you." Stanley Cosek craned over his shoulder to shout into his speakerphone. His back was to the telephone as he leaned over a pile of notes on his well-stocked desk.

"We're doing a series of articles, and we'd like to include you." The voice was high, but resonant with confidence. "We want to find out why some companies are achieving their quality and productivity goals, while others are just not making it, in spite of the advice they're getting from people like you."

"People like me," Stanley muttered, raising his tangled eyebrows. He moved over to the telephone and picked up the receiver. "You're asking the wrong question," he said. "Quality and productivity are results, not goals."

"Thank you," said the voice on the other end, suddenly sounding much nearer. "I was having a hard time hearing you, too. Let me explain. We want to find out what quality consultants are offering, and how companies are benefiting from their expertise."

"So why me?" Stanley was wondering how he could be considered representative of quality consultants, as this journalist seemed to imply.

"You have long experience and a good track record," came the brisk reply. "I'd like a day, if you can manage that. I'm sure you're aware that you're a controversial figure and we'd like to help our readers understand a little more about you. The publication is planning five or six profiles. We want to show what each quality consultant has to offer."

"You're certainly an optimist." Stanley did a quick review of his mental calendar. "I have a very full schedule. The only way I can give you more time is if you're willing to accompany me on my next business trip. I'll be happy to talk to you when I can. But things will be tight."

"When will that be?"

"There's a trip starting tomorrow. Let's see . . . I'll be catching the red-eye to Cleveland tomorrow night. I'll spend a day there, followed by two days in Minneapolis. Then, down to Dallas. It's my best offer."

There was silence on the other end. Stanley had the impression that another conversation was going on, out of earshot. Presumably, she was getting the go-ahead from her editor. He twirled his chair back to his notes on the desk opposite, switching back to the speakerphone. Then the voice came back, a little hollow. "Okay. That'll suit me just fine. A chance to watch you working with clients is exactly what I need."

"If you can get seats on the necessary flights . . ." Stanley replied, a cautionary note in his voice reflecting doubts that were settling on the surface of his mind. He suddenly wondered if he were making a big mistake. With a trip as demanding as this one, he needed to be absolutely focused on the tasks at hand. These included a talk at a seminar for managers, two days of consulting with a regular client, and a meeting with a huge and prestigious potential client. He needed all his wits about him if he was to assess the prospects of working successfully with this new company. Distraction, in the form of an inquisitive journalist, would not help.

"I may not be able to see you at all on Friday, which means you'll be at loose ends for a day," he added.

"You haven't said anything yet to scare me off," the reply came back. "And, there's no such thing as loose ends for a journalist."

"Hold on a minute. I'll put you through to my secretary, Judith. She can give you details of the flights."

There was a pause as Stanley tapped into his secretary's line. It was busy. Waiting for it to clear, he leafed over to a page of notes he'd made about a client company a couple of months back. He pulled it out and looked at it. The notes contained evidence of a phenomenon he was noticing more and more in his work: an enormous increase in improvements throughout a company after it had reduced complexity in a few areas. It was as if a medicine prescribed to cure one area of the body had acted as a tonic on the patient's whole system.

Stanley had been trying to think of a term to describe this remarkable phenomenon. As he tapped through to Judith's line again and she answered, it came to him: synchronous events.

Waiting with the receiver to her ear, Zara Morse swiveled her chair around to face a co-writer, who was sitting at the next desk in the office of *Business West,* the first Seattle-based business publication with national distribution. "I think I've got him—and for four days. I should be able to nail him in that time. Much better than an interview—lots of opportunity to find out what's really going on."

She turned back as Judith's voice came on the line with the schedule. Moments later, they both put down their phones. As Zara dialed through to her editor, Judith turned to Stanley and remarked, "This is a great opportunity for some press recognition. You don't usually go after it, Stanley, and you deserve to have some come to you. Especially from a publication like *Business West.*" She straightened the paper around the roller in her printer, pressed a key, and set it going.

Stanley looked uncertain. "I hope you're right. I seem to remember *Business West* recently ran an uncomplimentary article about consultants. They may be out for more evidence. I don't want to serve myself up on a platter if they're determined to give us a bad rap. This trip is complicated enough without harassment from a journalist."

"It'll sure be a test of endurance under pressure," Judith agreed. "If you can give a talk, do an audit, hold two full sessions with clients, fly five thousand miles, and provide some journalist with enough information to do a good article, all in the space of four days, you'll . . ." she hesitated.

". . . deserve a weekend off?" Stanley finished.

"About time, too." Judith fished the sheet of paper out of the printer. "Here. Everything's down—hotels, flight times, appointments."

Stanley glanced at it. As far as he could see, there was no slack anywhere. No room for any wasted time or energy. After years of applying his own principles of removing flaws from and reducing complexity in his schedule, he seldom had to worry about anything except the unpredictability of airplanes. But the presence of a journalist could disrupt his well-tuned schedule.

"Zara Morse may turn out to be something I could do without," he groaned, returning to his desk.

Judith smiled. "Well, you've been known to deal with complications deftly before now. You're sure to handle this one just fine."

***

Showing his card to the receptionist in the Red Carpet Lounge for frequent flyers, Stanley said, "I'm expecting someone to join me here. Please page me when she arrives."

Sitting down on one of the lounge's well-stuffed chairs, Stanley glanced over at the coffee machine to see how fresh the pot looked. In spite of his almost weekly flights, the limbo of the airport always left him feeling helpless and out of control. Deciding that the coffee looked over-brewed, he opened his briefcase and got out some papers. Their quiet shuffle had a way of imposing order on life, even in a place like this.

He was so deep in consideration of current problems in the tennis-racket division of his client in Minnesota that he hardly distinguished his name from the constant boom of announcements coming over the paging system.

Jumping up as it was repeated, he stepped into the reception area. Zara was standing between two cases and a tape recorder, looking intently toward the door into the lounge. She was wearing jeans and looked younger than her voice had led Stanley to expect. As he approached, she smiled with practiced confidence and held out her hand.

"I always travel as comfortably as I can on red-eye flights," she said. "Don't worry, I'll look more respectable when we visit your clients."

Stanley was already regretting his own discomfort, and his suitcases overburdened with suits, shirts, and ties. With a mind that constantly pondered other people's organizational problems, he himself was the one element that sometimes got left out of the calculations.

"I've been seriously considering throwing convention out with my formal clothes and resorting once and for all to Hawaiian shirts," Stanley replied as they sat down. "People might not associate them with serious work, but my ability to think creatively takes a quantum leap when I don't have a striped silk noose knotted around my neck."

Zara's expression was a mixture of delight and surprise. Stanley made a mental note to remember that everything he said from this moment could be written down in evidence against him. Journalists loved to make penetrating points about people's mode of dress, which he felt was his weakest point. His casual comment was sure to end up somewhere, sounding significant.

Zara's first question confirmed his suspicion. "Presumably your choice of clothes is all part of your self-marketing, isn't it?" she asked knowingly. "Like your talk tomorrow in Cleveland."

Stanley had to suppress a strong desire to remind Zara that he had granted her this interview. Why should he give her hours of his time if it didn't offer him at least a potential publicity benefit? But he decided to let it pass and answer the question at face value. After all, he was committed to her almost constant presence for four days, and they had better not start off on the wrong foot.

"As a matter of fact, dress doesn't mean beans to me," he replied, "though I know it does to a lot of people. And sure, I do have to market myself, just as other information providers have to. I believe in what I'm selling, so why shouldn't I want people who can benefit from it to know about it?" Already, he feared, he was sounding defensive, although he had nothing to be defensive about.

"Doctors, lawyers, and university professors sell their skills and they get themselves known," he went on, "through the press and in their writing. People need to know who they are, and what they have to offer. A seminar or talk is a perfect vehicle for me. People can size me up at close quarters. It's fairer than asking them to buy my goods on the phone or through the mail."

Zara took the cue. "So tell me about your goods. Why would a company want to buy them?"

Hit the big questions right off the bat, thought Stanley. This journalist wasn't one to pussyfoot around.

"A consultant," he said, pausing to gather his thoughts, "is one kind of information provider in a society where information carries more power than armies. Our strengths are information and objectivity, something most people within a company can't get at any price. All companies specialize, and most cannot generate their own information about everything they need to know. Consultants can also operate freely for the best interests of the company, without the bias that comes from internal positioning and politics."

Zara was scribbling in a ring-bound notebook. She nodded. "So what's the knowledge you're offering?"

"You'll be finding that out," Stanley replied, trying to sound bland. "You've got four days, you know. That should answer a few questions." He wondered how he could function at this level of inquisitional heat. Then he thought of a way of deflecting it for a while.

"You know, I'm giving a talk at the seminar tomorrow," he said. "I'd like to read it over to you. I haven't given it a practice run yet."

Zara nodded. "I do some public speaking, so I might be able to help a little. What's the subject?"

"It's about teamwork. Getting the whole company to work under the same baton."

"And are consultants like you the conductors who wield the baton?"

Stanley pondered a moment, then said, "Zara . . ." He had already decided that they might as well start off on first-name terms if they were to spend four days together. "Please realize the phrase 'like you' is meaningless when you talk about consultants in process control. No two of us are exactly alike. In some cases, what we're offering is diametrically opposed. People hear the word 'quality' and they think they know what it's all about. It's an idea that takes on many different guises and you have to know which one you're looking at."

He hoped Zara had done enough homework to know the fundamental differences in schools of thought between quality and process control specialists. Her expression gave nothing away, but he suddenly wanted to give her as much information as she could handle, if only to stop the flood of questions.

"Some quality consultants apply the ideas of Frederick Taylor, who has dominated our industry for almost a century now. Taylor did a lot to improve America's efficiency. But his methods aren't appropriate for today's world, even though there's still a large market for his principles. Others, like me, base our work on the paradigms of W. Edwards Deming, who taught the Japanese many of the techniques that have brought them so far."

Their flight was called, and they started toward the departure gate. Stanley found himself worrying about the materials necessary for his audit meeting on the last day of the trip. Which suitcase were they in? "You seem to be traveling light," he remarked to Zara. "I hate carrying so much baggage, but it always seems to be necessary when I visit several places on one trip."

"Could you rent a locker in Chicago and dump what you need for later events until you come through again? We're scheduled through Chicago at least twice, aren't we?"

"Scheduled, yes," Stanley said, with a sarcastic laugh. "But I never presume on the reliability of airline schedules. There's never any way to be sure where I'll find myself on the way to my stated destination."

"That sounds awkward," said Zara.

"It is. But it's one of the hazards of this way of life. As a consultant, I'm supposed to appear magically wherever and whenever I'm needed. The horrible truth is, I live life just like everyone else. My luggage gets lost, I get tired out by delays, and I worry."

"Welcome to the human race," said Zara, who was relieved to find Stanley Cosek, this gray eminence of the quality movement, so normal.

***

"How long have you been at *Business West?*" Stanley asked when they were seated in the plane.

"Just under a year. I came there from the *Portland Post,* an evening paper."

"That was quite a big jump, if you don't mind my saying so."

"I won an award for investigative reporting. I think that helped. It was a local business scam that got out of hand. *Sixty Minutes* followed it up, so it got national coverage. I'll send you a copy of it, if you're interested."

She switched the microphone on and said firmly, "But let's get back to your business. There's hardly a company in this country that doesn't pay lip service to quality and process control. So why aren't they achieving what they expect? With all the knowledge available to them, surely we ought to be brimming with successful businesses that put the Japanese and Koreans back in the shade."

Stanley peered with distaste at the microphone hooked over the armrest between them. Takeoff always left him feeling tense. "Theories are only the beginning. Why do we find it so hard to exercise, or give up smoking, even when we know all the arguments?" he replied, wondering why he couldn't cut down on caffeine, and wishing desperately for a cup of strong coffee. "It's just the same, but magnified a hundred times in a company. Change is threatening."

"But companies are always issuing directives for people to do things in new ways. Isn't change a survival skill, in nature as well as in the corporate world?"

"Certainly. But people get very upset about the prospect of making major changes, especially if they have to shift their attitudes. It's easier for them to blame problems on someone or something else: the economy, another department, trade laws. Many companies make surface changes, which give an impression of progress. But changes are meaningless unless companies become more competitive and continue that trend. Remedies in a spray-can are tempting, and many companies fall for them. But real change happens on a deeper level and takes more time. That's the kind I try to teach."

Stanley craned his head to look up the aisle. The beverage cart was finally lumbering towards them.

"So what makes people accept what you have to offer?" Zara asked. "The kind of remedies that take time to cook, rather than the canned variety?"

"The best motivation is desperation," Stanley came back. "That's where the Japanese were when Deming arrived among them after the war. And look where it got them. Yes, crisis has its virtues. It gets people moving, as long as they don't give way to helplessness. That's why I'm working at the best time possible. I'll have a coffee, please."

Zara accepted a diet cola, and turned to look at him in surprise.

"When people are prosperous, they get lazy. They see no reason to change. 'If it ain't broke, don't fix it' is a convenient little catchphrase dreamed up by a nation having a self-satisfied snooze. But I'm saying, Fix it now, because even though it may not be broken, Japan or some other competitor will run right by us if we don't. Doing okay is no longer good enough. Improvement must be continuous."

Stanley paused to down some coffee. Zara jumped in: "But there are many consultants saying this, and selling advice and techniques for high prices. How's a potential client to know who will really deliver the goods?"

"True, there's a lot on offer. But you know, all consultants have track records that are freely available for scrutiny. They offer what they offer. It's up to the client to match their needs with a particular consultant. Prices vary, but once the client is teamed with a consultant who can really make a difference, the payoff should become more apparent than the cost.

"As for my specialties," Stanley went on, after a moment's

pause, "well, they may not look so thrilling at first glance. I don't sell tapes or software or how-to books. Though I give talks, I don't put on high-powered weekend seminars. My job is to go into companies and work with them to find flaws in their systems. Not very glamorous, really. It's hard work. It can cause pain. We often have to do major surgery on systems that are not functioning well."

"Doesn't that cause a lot of disruption?"

"The first thing we have to do is make people realize that the system is the cause of their difficulties, not their own incompetence. We also have to move them away from the common idea that technology is the remedy, or that a new set of motivational tricks will get people going. These things may help, but they're never enough on their own."

"So, what's the answer?" asked Zara.

"The key is removing flaws in the system," Stanley replied. "To do that, we must observe by measuring what we have, make alterations, and measure again, until things start moving in the right direction. Everyone gets involved. We have to help people look at things in a new way. They have to learn to stop blaming people for failures, and look dispassionately at the way the system is designed. It's painful in a way; a bit like an unpleasant medicine. But it's simple and comparatively inexpensive. And it's the remedy that makes the company competitive."

"But it's a process, not a pill," said Zara. Stanley looked at her and smiled. He was pleased that she'd already grasped this important point.

"Absolutely right. There's nothing instant about the kind of help I offer. It spreads health through a company the way preventive medicine promotes health in a body, by enabling it to utilize its own strength. The effects can sometimes be dramatic, but that depends on the kind of flaw we're removing. I don't advertise quick fixes."

"The effects of preventive medicine are hard to measure," observed Zara. "How do you gauge your results?"

"As a statistician, I do a lot of measuring, and I teach others to do it all the time. It's like taking the company's temperature and observing its rise and fall over a long period. We can tell a great deal from that. If a specific remedy causes an observable change, we know we're on to something."

The plane was cruising steadily by now, above clouds that seemed to be growing denser and darker. Stanley gazed intently out of the window for a few moments. He sounded contemplative when he added, "But there's an overall health that sometimes returns to a company after we've been working together for some time. I've seen surges of improvement that I can't quite explain, because they happen in areas where nobody has worked specifically. I call them synchronous events."

It was the first time Stanley had mentioned this phrase since he coined it, and he paused a moment with the realization that he might truly have discovered something. "These changes are hard to measure, and I can't take credit for them directly. But I believe they're related to what we've done."

He reached into his briefcase. "And now I'd like you to listen to my speech." For the next hour or so he talked, referring occasionally to a paper headed, "Getting a Team Together." It was apparent that this was not a rehearsed speech, but one that he was rethinking as he spoke the words. The coffee cart rolled by, and he paid no attention to it.

When the captain asked them to fasten their seat belts for the descent, Stanley peered out once more at the flawless blue sky that ended below the aircraft in ominous billows of heavy cloud. "Hopelessness covers us like a thick fog down there," he commented. "But it's unnecessary really, because up here the view is lovely. All we need is to get out from under the clouds for long enough to see the possibilities. That's what a consultant is for. We see the possibilities, and point the way. We're optimistic realists, you see."

***

Down below, at O'Hare, the possibilities were clouded for even the most optimistic. The 8:05 A.M. plane that was to have carried them on to Cleveland was grounded by bad weather several hundred miles to the west.

"I should have expected it," Stanley muttered, as he went

off to find a telephone. "We won't be into Cleveland now in time to take a break before my talk. I'll have to grab some rest on the flight. We'll miss lunch altogether."

They arrived at the majestic Frank Lloyd Wright building just outside Cleveland, half an hour after the scheduled time for Stanley's talk. The time-zone change compounded the time loss. Ushered in by one of the organizers, Stanley took the podium without delay in front of a gathering of some three hundred middle- and upper-level managers.

"Since I've done the unforgivable for a consultant in process control, and have failed to be just-in-time, I am going to address the issue that is uppermost in my mind instead of the one scheduled." To Stanley's relief, his pun raised a laugh, that helped to counteract any negative reactions to his announcement.

"You can read my ideas on teamwork in the conference proceedings. I'll touch on the subject, and answer any questions you have at the end of the session. But now, I want to address something different: operating a company in the face of unexpected events."

Looking up in surprise, Zara realized she would not be able to sit back through this one. The rehearsal she got on the plane was no rehearsal. A new production is about to begin, she thought.

For the next hour, Stanley addressed the daunting question of how to run a business in light of the scientific discovery that events cannot be regarded as a simple chain of causes and effects. Business, he pointed out, has not caught up with the momentous growth of understanding in the world of physics. Yet these discoveries call into question the cause-and-effect mentality that still dominates the world of management and manufacturing. In this context, both financial forecasting and company planning, which occupy hundreds of the best brains and cost billions of dollars a year, could be considered wasted resources. With a regularity that is the only predictable thing about them, unforeseen events wipe out the grand plans of the best business minds.

"Detailed planning for the future is obsolete," Stanley told his audience. "Our minds are set in the mode of a nineteenth-century cosmology, which assumes that everything can be determined if we have enough information. So we spend our time in research and data-gathering, filling our files and our minds with projections and calculations that will almost certainly never turn out as we expected—because the unexpected is an inevitable part of everything we do.

"We need to start living in the present by observing how well our systems are working. We must train our minds to observe the facts. By working closely with this raw material—the operations in our organizations and industries—we can find and remove flaws to let the system keep moving toward the height of its potential. By reducing the complexity of what we have, instead of creating complexities for the future, we're better prepared to handle the unexpected."

Stanley talked about practical ways to reduce complexity. He demonstrated how to gather data on the status quo rather than an abstract future. He told his audience how the old idea of division of labor takes on new life when a company catches on to the idea of reducing complexity.

"When something in the environment changes, we can detect it more quickly. We can make adjustments to the system faster because we understand it thoroughly, through measurements and statistics. If we don't, we could be left hanging on to elaborately devised plans that are suddenly irrelevant."

At the end of his talk, Stanley fielded almost an hour of questions and discussion. He seemed to have touched on a highly sensitive collective nerve.

Toward the conclusion of the session, a young man stood up, and asked: "Mr. Cosek, I read your article on teamwork in the proceedings. But what's going to motivate managers to take a company through the kind of change you advocate? The qualities that get a person into a managerial position—drive, ambition, self-confidence—seem to have no place in your scheme of things."

"It all comes down to the difference between good managers and good leaders," replied Stanley. "People have been discussing the elements of good management since Machiavelli wrote *The Prince*. We've tried theories X, Y, and Z. But we still don't thoroughly understand the meaning of leadership, or how to select leaders. It's obvious that our companies need this commodity as much as they need their raw materials. But they may have been looking in the wrong place for it. It turns out that leaders and managers are not necessarily the same thing."

As he spoke, Stanley realized the questioner had touched on one of the trickiest areas of his work; a question he was still struggling with himself: how to find leaders strong enough to take organizations through the boulder-strewn paths of real change. This was a subject for another lecture, a seminar, or even a conference. But it needed fresh minds and a willingness to explore the subject from different angles.

Stanley looked at the moderator, who held up five fingers. "If you want me to get into this one in five minutes, don't be surprised if I say some outrageous things. These are deep and turbulent waters." He took a deep breath, and found himself swaying alarmingly, as if his feet could no longer be trusted to hold him up.

"Finding the right leaders to work with me in pushing a company through the inevitable struggle toward superb corporate health is probably my biggest challenge. Good leaders are like guides in the wilderness. They're willing to be out front even though they may not have covered the track themselves. They are risk-takers; change-makers.

"On the other hand, I frequently meet managers who are totally unwilling to change, and these are often the people who end up in positions of high authority. They've learned to play the game and to win. But that's not necessarily the same thing as making the company a winner. Someone with less political skill, who in our system seldom gets to the top, might have been a much healthier choice for the company."

The moderator looked at the clock. It was approaching the five-minute mark. Stanley, exhausted by a sleepless night and the frustrations of the day, looked out over the heads in the lecture hall, and addressed the area of darkness where the question had emerged. "This could be one of the most important questions of all. I'm glad you raised the point. We need to know how to select people who will make good leaders. Thank you all for your attention and participation."

Stanley found himself suddenly stumbling off the stage, like a man already drowning in sleep. For a moment, he could hardly remember where he was or what he had been talking about. As the audience broke up, little explosions of comment or protest burst here and there. The organizer caught him by the arm, shaking it and congratulating him. "Very interesting lecture. Most thought-provoking," he pronounced, in the voice of one who has said the same words many times before. "I hope you will join us in the lounge for cocktails."

"Great idea," said Stanley, beginning to feel like an automaton. "But you know, I was on an airplane most of last night. Why don't I join you a little later?"

Somebody took him to his room. Zara found her way to the lounge and listened intently to the conversations around her, taking notes on a small white pad.

An hour later, she excused herself from a conversation with a junior executive from Indiana, and slipped out to find a pay phone. It was late afternoon in Seattle, and she caught her editor just before he was due to go into an editorial meeting about next month's features.

"Josh, just checking in. I've heard Cosek speak. He certainly provoked his audience. He's got a very wide perspective on his subject—more than we thought, though he seemed stumped by a question from the floor. He's really a bit of an enigma."

"Just keep digging. It's the results we're interested in. Watch him carefully when he's in action."

"Tomorrow I should have a chance for that. I've been talking to some of the managers here. Clearly, Cosek is a guy who gets results. Huge reductions in defects, turnaround times, cost of goods sold. A lot of people here admit that, even though they're put off by some of his comments on managers. There seems to be a general opinion that he demands too much of his clients."

"Make sure you get him to reply to those views. Must go. I'm late for the meeting."

Zara looked doubtfully at her notes. "Josh, hold it. I'm not sure this Cosek is going to deliver the kind of investigative article you have in mind."

"Zara, this is your first day. Don't be taken in by his words. Most of these guys look plausible enough. They're good salesmen; they have to be. But remember, we have reason to believe that some of them are doing actual damage, and damaged companies mean lost jobs and slowing economies. It's important that we expose people who are misguiding our businesses."

"Josh, I think he's the genuine . . ." Zara, normally so confident, suddenly felt overwhelmed by the enormity of her task; ". . . article," she finished faintly.

"Yeah, you'll get a good article," came the reply, as the line started to crackle. "Watch his actions. Look at people's faces in the company you're visiting tomorrow. Get hard evidence about results. Modern gods usually turn out to have feet of clay— you'll see." And he hung up.

***

Before Stanley sank into sleep, he took the precaution of telephoning the airline and booking Zara and himself on an earlier flight to Minneapolis. Next morning, his alarm shrilled at five o'clock and he phoned through to Zara's room.

"We'll have to be out of here at six sharp," he told Zara, his voice dour with unfinished sleep. "I'm not risking any delays today."

As the plane leveled out and headed toward Minnesota, Zara pulled out her electronic paraphernalia and said, "Okay, please fill me in on Zeeback, Inc."

"D'you play tennis?" asked Stanley.

"I used to. Don't much now. This job takes up my weekends and evenings so I usually get my exercise by racing out to one of those wild classes where I can shout as well as jump around before I go back to the office."

"Well, then, you buy shoes for that?"

"Sure do. They cost a fortune too, especially the ones with gimmicks like inflatable soles, or air vents, or extra colored laces."

"Exactly. It's those little gimmicks that are causing the problems I'm dealing with now at Zeeback. The marketing people want them pronto; as soon as they see the demand. And they want them cheap. The manufacturing people are having a hard time making marketing see that these little details are costly in materials, setup, and lead time. I'm trying to find ways to satisfy both. I'll show you some examples when we're there. It's better for you to see this kind of ongoing process in action than for me to try and describe it. Like anything that involves change, it's hard to describe while it's in process."

"So what about the tennis rackets?"

"That's a success story, so it's an easy one to tell. Zeeback makes four grades of rackets, each under a different name. There's the standard, strung; and the premium, unstrung. Then there's the custom racket, which carries the name of the store that strings and sells it; and a professional grade, made for individual pro players.

"When I came into this company two years ago, it was losing ground fast. They had changed to a new composite material for the rackets, a mix of resins and fiberglass. At that time, they inspected the rackets and did a few crude tests to make sure they were the right dimensions and weights. But they could never be sure the racket was good, or not until it was put to use.

"The standard grade, for example, often had flaws which didn't show up until it was strung. Once it was strung, it couldn't be economically reworked, and that meant it was thrown out. The premium-grade racket was strung in the stores, but some customers started coming back, complaining that different parts of the face were performing differently. Since the rackets bore the names of the stores, their reputation was going down the drain. They were furious, as you can imagine."

"How about the pros?"

"These were essentially the same rackets as the premiums. But because of the high defect rate, they had to be strung and sent out to individual players to try, dozens at a time. It was the only way to ensure a good fit. Only the rackets that were acceptable to the pros could be used. The ones that were returned already strung couldn't be sold, so each rejected racket was costing the company thousands. They were only just managing to hang on to their reputation as well."

"So how did you save the situation?"

"We looked at the materials they were using for the frames. Slightly altered proportions in the ingredients made the frames a little more stable under pressure. We designed experiments with the heating and cooling cycles, and with the injection pressure for the molds, until we found the ones that gave us highest consistency. Everyone offered their input. It was a remarkable example of cooperation."

"How long did it take?"

"Almost a year, until we were sure there'd be no more surprises."

"A long time. Were people willing to wait that long?"

"Some people may have complained at the time. Most understood that we couldn't wave a wand. We had to take it step by step, remove one flaw at a time. But look what we've got now. Zeeback's tennis rackets were already considered top of the line. It will take them a little while to outlive that spell of poor quality when they switched to the new materials, but they are already gaining their public back."

Zeeback Inc., manufacturer of sports equipment, occupied a series of long, low buildings pleasantly situated in a green zone just outside Minneapolis. A rolling golf course was invitingly within view. Stanley and Zara walked through the plate-glass doors of the main building and were directed straight to the office of the manufacturing manager, Caleb Garth. He beamed as they entered, and held out his hand to Stanley.

"Stanley, I have to tell you the work we did last week has already paid dividends. We're getting the people in the stitching area to keep scores. They were nervous at first, but now it's turned into a game. The defect rate has already gone down, we can see just from a glance at their charts."

Stanley smiled benignly. No business trip can be all bad. Now he was getting yesterday's flip side, he thought.

"So what now?" he asked. "What's the latest bug in the system?"

Caleb looked at his watch. "The designers want to talk to you. I told them you might be able to go over there now. They're having problems keeping up with the rapid changes in styles. Marketing wants to step up the rate of new designs in joggers and exercise shoes, particularly women's. There seems to be an insatiable appetite for detail out there."

The three of them marched smartly down a series of corridors, lined with nouveau prints of athletes and sportsmen in artistic poses.

Stanley set to work with the designers, closely examining the arrangement of their hours, their tasks, and their deadlines. After observing the session for ten minutes, Zara slipped out.

A woman in a blue-check suit stopped her and asked if she was looking for anyone. Zara explained that she was researching an article on Zeeback's strategies for improving quality and productivity. She did not mention that she was traveling with Stanley Cosek, and to her surprise, the woman did not inquire about her initial contact.

Instead, she looked thoughtful for a moment, then said, "I think I know someone who could help you. Let me see if he's available. My name's Gayle Palumbo, by the way. I'm a marketing manager." She held out her hand.

Knocking on a door marked W.J. Goosens, Ms. Palumbo entered without pause. A man looked up from his desk and smiled warmly. Clearly more than just a colleague of Gayle's, thought Zara. "Wayne Goosens, product manager for tennis shoes," he said affably, shooting his hand across the desk toward Zara.

A look of relish appeared on Goosens' face as soon as he heard Zara's request. "Let me see," he looked at his watch. "I could probably manage half an hour now. Why don't you join us, Gayle? After all, you've had quite a bit to say about how efficiency in production affects marketing."

"I'm on my way down to manufacturing, but it shouldn't take long. I'll stop back in about fifteen minutes. Okay?" She turned on her elegant Italian heels and went out.

"I'm interested in finding out how Zeeback is coping with competition," said Zara, feigning innocence.

"Your question happens to be one that's occupying my mind quite a bit. Sports shoes are a hectic area; extremely competitive, with companies coming up with more and more innovations to grab consumers' attention."

He paused and looked hard at the photo of a Wimbledon finals match on his wall. "We have to be as nimble on our feet as any sportsman—changing tactics fast, bringing out new products every few months. Our R&D department is kept on its toes night and day. As product manager, I have to be ready to scuttle one style of shoe and bring out another at short notice, according to what the competition is doing, or the latest pronouncements of the health experts."

"Yet you have to maintain high quality and dependability through all the changes?" questioned Zara.

"That's the big challenge," said Goosens. "But a couple of directors have seen fit to bring in a quality consultant. He's spending a lot of time teaching everyone, from top executives to the machinists that sew tongues into the shoes, about linearity, reducing flaws; getting everyone to take statistics on what they're doing. These are terrific goals for a company that's just starting up, or one that is essentially producing the same product over and over. But we don't have time for that. We're market-driven. Our products are always changing. The people in production need to know only as much as they will use for their job, and be motivated to do it well. There's no point in overloading them with theories."

Gayle came in and sat down. "What Wayne may not have told you," she broke in, "is that Zeeback recently took over a company called Airtread, which specializes in sports shoes. Before that, Zeeback had a very small shoe division that was part of a wide range of sporting goods. But footwear has become one of the hottest sports items, and Zeeback was anxious to expand into that field." She looked at Wayne. He continued.

"Gayle and I both moved over here from Airtread. We're very familiar with this field, and had our production going without a hitch before the takeover. But changing to a completely different system is eroding our efficiency. And our profitability." Wayne practically spat out the last sentence.

Gayle took over, apparently anxious not to appear too critical. "What Stanley Cosek's doing is very idealistic," she continued, as if she and Wayne had been over these arguments many times before. "But we frankly don't have time for idealism. We need a system we can put straight into place; something which will help our workers keep up with the changes, not something that will confuse them."

"Some are confused, but others are picking up Cosek only too well," Wayne interjected. "What we don't need is an over-sophisticated work force who back-talk to us about low scrap-rates and low inventories. Their job is to make product, not tell us about quality."

When Zara left Goosens' office, her mind was doing somersaults. His complaint was the opposite of the one she'd expected when she first planned the story. As far as she could see it, Stanley Cosek was offending Goosens and Palumbo by being too thorough and wanting to achieve real health in the company. Yet maybe his demand for change at a deep level was simply unrealistic. If they wanted an instant cure, was it necessarily to the detriment of the company's long-term health? Or was Stanley's idealism a solid basis for an energetic leap into the future?

***

"Today was a humdinger for me," Stanley told Zara on the drive back to the hotel. He was beaming. "One of those occasions when one gets tangible results almost immediately. Unusual, but it can happen. I call it gathering the low-hanging fruit."

"Tell me about it," said Zara, preparing for another onslaught of evidence for her files.

"Well, we gained a more thorough understanding of something that was just a sense of growing pressure and chaos before. These researchers are under pressure to keep up with a rapidly changing and unpredictable market demand," Stanley said.

"But it's more complicated than just keeping up with the latest fads. It's a case of clarifying goals, maybe even market positioning. The marketing people want to be highly responsive to the customer; ahead of the competition in fashion and style developments. But Zeeback was known as a manufacturer of dependable but rather dull, economically priced sports shoes before the Airtread people came into the picture."

"I don't really see why all this concerns a quality consultant," said Zara. "Isn't your job simply to make sure they remain dependable?"

"Precisely," said Stanley. "But that requires more than tinkering with production lines. It means helping people to define their goals and roles. The conflict between the pressure to produce novelties and the need to keep quality standards high causes confusion, and consequently, more complexity. There's a third pressure, too." He paused.

Zara smiled. Stanley had a professorial quality about him, and she knew he wanted her to supply the answer like a good student. "Speed?" she suggested.

"True," said Stanley, "that's part of the need to keep up with fashion. But I was thinking of price. Zeeback wants to stay in the lower to middle price range. Changes in style are very expensive. That means the production workers have to be highly skilled and quick to catch problems. They have to understand the importance of rapid turnover of inventory and the most efficient way to organize a production line. You don't pay these people the lowest wages."

"So how does this affect the designers?"

"Well, we discovered today, after making charts of the way they spend their time, that almost a third of it is evaporating in meetings called to review the latest doings of the competition: another area where complexity is running rampant. But high fashion and high quality both cost money in materials, in testing, packaging, documentation, and frequent organizational changes. The only way to absorb all these costs is by reducing complexity, finding flaws in the system and rooting them out."

"Reducing scrap and inventory?" Zara inquired, her face like a poker.

"That and a lot of other things which a well-trained work force can do successfully with the right guidance. The higher cost of a skilled work force is easily outweighed by the savings we achieve—tens of thousands, sometimes, as a result of one well-aimed change."

"And the designers; what must they change?"

"Our meeting this morning helped them clarify many of the points I've just told you. Finding out exactly where their time's been going gave them solid evidence on which to base changes."

"Did it take a special visit from a consultant to make them realize they were going to meetings too often?" asked Zara, trying to hold on to her skepticism.

"Like most important discoveries, it was too obvious for them to see," Stanley came back firmly. "And coming to grips with their problems helped us understand others at the same time. It shone a bright light on the biggest problem of all—the company's inability to resolve the question of market position."

"Trying to be all things to all feet?"

"If you like. People often know something isn't right, but they can't quite pinpoint the cause. Someone has to take a surgical knife to old habits; cut them open and expose them for what they are. If you lay bare facts on the table and examine them objectively, without explanations or excuses, it's surprising what can be done with them. The presence of a consultant gives people the license to examine the old assumptions, and start making changes."

"It sounds a little like the work of a shrink."

"In a way, you're right. It's a bit of everything, this job: statistician, doctor, piano teacher, analyst. Sometimes revelations come with apparently very little effort. Meetings like the one I had today can seem like gathering low-hanging fruit. But you only get that if you've prepared the ground first. Sometimes results take far longer: months, even years before the idea is fully taken on board and used efficiently. I'll show you some examples tomorrow."

***

By the end of the next day, Zara knew more about the manufacture of tennis rackets than she ever imagined possible. She had already decided which model she wanted for herself, and found herself thinking about people she might persuade to play some games after work or on weekends.

She had also been able to understand, in a more concrete way, what Stanley was getting at when he talked about reducing flaws in the system. She observed him, sleeves rolled up, talking with line workers over great vats of resin or huge molding machines, gesticulating to make his point clearer above the din.

Corrinne, who worked in racket stringing, showed Zara the charts that seemed to spring up in every corner like mushrooms. "It's a kind of game for us now. It's fun keeping score on our own areas—makes the job more interesting."

"Don't people worry about incriminating themselves? I mean, if your area scores low, aren't you called down about it?"

"We used to be nervous, and it's taken a while to believe we won't be blamed if things aren't as perfect as they should be. But Stanley's taught us all a different reflex: Look for the flaws in the system, not in each other."

Waldo, the supervisor, explained things more theatrically. "People come up to Stanley and say, 'We have this terrible problem.' Stanley replies, 'That's nice, but show me some data.' 'What kind of data d'you want?' 'Well, let me show you how to collect some useful data,' says Stanley. They measure some aspect of the process that's causing problems. Maybe it's the speed of a conveyor belt, or the temperature of this fiberglass soup we have over here."

Waldo gestured in the direction of the material used to make racket frames. Then he went on, "So Stanley says, 'Put a dot on this chart to represent the measurement we just got. Then do the same thing tomorrow, and every day. I'll be back in a week.' When he gets back, he says, 'Tell me what was happening when the dot was up here . . . and down there. You do the job, so you ought to know.' This way, they start to figure out exactly what's going on when things are going right, and what's going on when they're not. They make some adjustments in the system, and watch what happens to the charts. This way, they slowly understand what's going on, and they start making improvements."

"Isn't it tedious?" asked Zara.

"No way. Watching the dots, figuring out what they mean, makes the job more interesting. It gives us something to think about, a real handle on the job. It's catching. Fellow employees look at what's been done and say, 'How did you do that? Well gee, maybe I could measure something over here.' Most people end up feeling more committed, because they're making a real difference. In some cases, they're taking over the engineer's task. That frees the engineers up to get on with what they're really good at. We don't need them or the quality inspectors around here the way we used to."

"How so?"

"Everyone's become a quality inspector," said Waldo, with a grin.

Many of the improvements in the racket division were well established, but Stanley insisted on measurements to keep operations running at maximum efficiency. "You never stop improving," he would say, "and there's no point of diminishing returns."

***

Sitting at dinner that evening in the plush dining room of the hotel, Stanley felt oddly ill at ease with his companion, though by now he had spent two full days and a whole waking night with her. Going from complete lack of knowledge to this forced intimacy was taking a bigger toll on his patience than he had expected.

He really wanted to eat alone tonight. Normally, after a day with Zeeback, letting his mind wander through this pink and mint-green dining room was one of the pleasures of his biweekly trips to Minneapolis. Occasionally he had dinner with someone from the company, but more often he was happy to unwind on his own. Observing the other lone travelers like himself, overhearing the conversations of the groups and couples, most of whom probably knew one another well, had become a favorite pastime.

He had to make an effort to conceal the irritation in his voice when replying to the first question of the evening.

"Are you any clearer about the question of leadership?" Zara asked. "I heard people discussing that one after the lecture. A lot of them seemed puzzled." Looking up from his vichyssoise, he saw that she was looking at him with an expression a cat might wear before pouncing on a bird: a combination of savagery and fondness. He thought a moment before shoveling a too-big spoonful into his mouth.

"Remember, Zara," he said, with a tone of something more than firmness. "I don't sell recipe books. Like many people who are interested in their work, I'm constantly learning too. I'm not afraid of admitting I don't know something. Contradictions and inconsistencies don't bother me, either. They're valuable pointers. They let me know what I don't know."

Zara was dissecting huge prawns, described on the menu as "swimming in a provocative lime and ginger dressing."

"Sounds like something out of *Alice in Wonderland.* But you might have to explain that." The tape recorder, as usual, occupied the third place at the table.

"I'll do my best," Stanley answered, thinking that whatever his starter, he would be unlikely to respond to provocation in this setting. "As I've told you, I supply information. I constantly collect data and distill that into a body of knowledge that's always growing and changing."

A T-bone steak and a grilled sole touched down momentarily on the white tablecloth, and were reversed as the waiter realized he had the order the wrong way around.

"Questions are part of a two-way transaction. The ones I can't answer are my personal reward. After all, the content of my lectures is no surprise to me." Stanley looked with some regret at Zara's plate. "A good question gives me a bone to chew on."

Zara looked up and smiled. Good quotes were a treat for her, just as a good question was to Stanley, she reflected.

Carefully removing the backbone in one piece from his sole, Stanley went on. "You know, I could go into a company and sell them a fish. They would probably be pleased, because it would be a tangible item, like this very good specimen."

He ate a forkful and nodded appreciatively. "It would go down well, because a fish is a simple thing. It doesn't require much skill to eat, and you feel better for a short while afterwards. But ultimately it doesn't make the company any healthier. It just makes them dependent on the consultant for another fish. What's more, the darned thing could be freeze-dried and identical to the one he's selling the next company, though he'll try to convince them it was caught exclusively for them.

"I try to offer information that's alive and still thrashing. It requires more effort to pin down, true. But it's living knowledge, different for each situation. After that, the challenge is to teach the clients how to catch fish themselves. But that means committing themselves to the uncomfortable process of learning and changing. This is where leadership comes in. The people who can take a company safely through this phase are the leaders. One of my jobs is to ferret them out and work with them."

Zara nodded and scribbled. After a moment she asked, "But how long does all this take? Surely most companies don't have time to wait for slow changes. They are in a fast-changing market. They're also up against heavy competition. The sports shoe market for example—I see it in the stores. There's always something new. Aren't your ideas a bit idealistic for this world?"

"Not if they work. The idea of synchronous events sounds improbable, but that doesn't mean it's not happening, any more than gravity didn't happen before Newton put a name to it. Once you start reducing complexity in a company, paring away the flaws in several areas, other things start happening too. You get a multiplicity of improvements you didn't even try to engineer. I can't say I really understand how or why it happens." He paused, and with a meaningful look added, "Certainly Wayne Goosens hasn't grasped the idea, as I'm sure you've found out."

Zara felt her temperature rise, though her face registered nothing. She refused to be made to feel embarrassment about doing her job. It was vital that she take in the opposition's point of view as well as Cosek's, even though she was traveling in his camp.

"Certainly," she said defiantly. "It's important for me to get as many different viewpoints as I can."

"Of course. But let me try to explain as best I can. In a manufacturing organization, when we reduce complexity, we start to see the organism behaving as a whole rather than a series of parts. I've seen it happening too many times now to dismiss it as coincidence. The most recent example is Carwell, a company in Orange County, California, which I've been working with for over a year. Some of the changes hardly seem explicable in the normal terms of cause and effect. It's exciting, because it's almost as if the changes we're accomplishing in one corner of the company are happening spontaneously elsewhere."

"Doesn't that sound a bit mystical for a man of science like you?"

"It's mysterious, certainly. But scientists are dealing with mysteries all the time. Physicists and biologists are ahead of manufacturers. Some are trying to understand the mechanism of communication that makes a whole school of fish turn with one impulse, or a flock of birds wing their way in one direction with a single intent. It's this kind of thing I sometimes think I'm experiencing when a company I work with is really latching on to the idea of reducing complexity."

Zara experienced a tremor of excitement. She hardly knew whether it was Stanley's words, or the excellent cabernet she was drinking. This was heady stuff, but was it anything more than words? Listening to a man whose thoughts went beyond politics, beyond money, beyond even the temporal success of his own ideas—this was a different order of experience from the bitter nit-picking conversation she'd had that afternoon with Wayne and Gayle. But she had little real proof that his ideas had any more permanent effect on a company's system than a good wine did on hers.

Stanley was still talking: "When you start reducing complexity, there's much more cooperation. People are not battling away solving unnecessary crises, for one thing. There's a simplicity; a clarity of purpose. The Japanese have known it for years."

"But Goosens and Gayle Palumbo didn't feel that. They felt your methods weren't working. They said things were going fine at their last plant," she said, making an effort to maintain a professional distance. "They gave me figures, so presumably they know what they're doing. Wouldn't you agree that their methods are as valid as yours?"

"They were getting results, certainly, in terms of output. I have to say Wayne and Gayle and their colleagues did a remarkable job of keeping things together as long as they did. But that was a very unhappy company. Internal strife was rampant. Staff turnover, particularly in production, was higher than they'd ever admit. The marketing people were making deals with stores, promising deliveries of new products on such short notice that manufacturing would be thrown into pandemonium.

"The company managed to make the deliveries because it was willing to pay high overtime on an hourly basis for people to come in and complete what couldn't be done during a normal working day. But its finances were in a mess. That's why it was taken over."

Zara sighed. She wished she were more expert at catching this man in an error. "If wages were good, why was turnover so high?"

"It was partly the constant atmosphere of chaos. And the quota system, which required people to do a certain pre-agreed amount, or else. If they didn't, they were automatically at fault, not the system. Sometimes people were working against tremendous odds, in a system that stymied them. They wanted to do well, but management was looking at their performance and judging it on a personal basis. I don't blame them. They were thinking the way most managers think in this country. I believe it would have been better to point less at the people, and more at the system to find out why people weren't achieving their quotas."

Stanley looked at his watch. "I need to get to my room. There's work to do before tomorrow, and it'll be another early start. You stay here and have dessert and coffee, if you like."

"None for you?"

"I'll skip it this time." He rose from his chair, then sat down again and leaned across the table slightly. "Remember, if my work succeeds, the two managers at Zeeback can't take personal credit for the improvements. It's very simple. I'm bad news for egotists. It's not that I take the credit instead. It's just that a new ethos comes into force—one where credit is not as important as a concerted effort to perfect the system, and keep perfecting it. That requires everyone's input, not just the managerial staff's."

He got up again, said goodnight and walked, a little stiffly, to the door. Zara looked at the menu and ordered crème caramel and coffee. Then she pulled out her notebook and started writing. Anyone looking over her shoulder would have noticed that her scribbles no longer bristled with question marks. She looked like a writer with a lot to say.

After twenty minutes, she wrote, "Tell Josh this may not make an investigative," and put a large asterisk beside it. Then she gulped down the last of her coffee and left the dining room.

***

The next day's flight took them via Milwaukee, instead of Chicago as originally planned. But they arrived in Dallas only half an hour later than scheduled. Stanley had already made it clear that Zara would have to occupy herself independently. Sitting in the back of the car en route to Wellco, the large and prestigious prospective client, Zara could see from Stanley's rigid posture in the front seat that he was nervous.

A marketing assistant called Dan took Zara around to some departments and introduced her to a range of people. She knew from what Stanley had told her that there were problems on a scale befitting an organization of five billion dollars a year.

Wellco's air of massive industrial might made it hard to imagine difficulties such as huge delays on production lines, late deliveries, high defect rates, and low morale. But, even as people tried to play down the scale of the problems, Zara picked up enough hints that all was not well in this bastion of American industry to convince her that Stanley's powers would be well tested here.

That evening, they climbed wearily onto the plane to Seattle. Stanley sat for a long time with his eyes closed, or staring out at the sky that seemed to be caught in an endless twilight as they chased the day back into the west.

After traveling together for so long, Zara felt it was appropriate to step outside the reporter-subject relationship and converse like two normal beings; at least for a few moments. In a casual tone, she asked, "How did it go today? D'you think you'll get the job?"

Stanley let out a sigh like a collapsing bellows; whether of weariness or frustration, it was hard to tell. He swiveled around from the porthole and looked straight at her.

"It's not a case of 'getting' the job. The manufacturing vice president is already clear that he wants me to work with him. He's well aware that I could save the company a great deal of money. The question is whether I want to take on the company."

Zara opened her eyes wide in surprise. "But I thought Wellco was the pick of the crop: that consultants have been playing leapfrog to get this one."

"That's true. It's an enormous, wealthy company, which creams off the best and brightest, as the press loves to call them, from the top management schools. Yet look at the mess it's in. Can you guess the reason for that?"

Zara, unaccustomed as she was, found herself feeling stupid. She couldn't answer.

"Well, there are probably two major reasons. One is that Wellco already has a vast quality control department."

"So they don't want you and you don't want them?"

"They sure don't think they need me. But think about it. The only time people are interested in brain surgery is when they have brain tumors. Yet if their heads hurt, they won't reach that logical conclusion, so they'll continue taking aspirin till they die. And that's what some of these in-house quality programs turn out to be: aspirins."

Zara laughed. "I get the picture," she said. "So what's the other reason?"

"The prevailing ethic of leadership in that company is one of brilliance hell-bent on outshining brilliance. Too many people want to be conductor."

"Egotists," commented Zara.

"It's trained into them," said Stanley. "There's an ideal image in America of the good manager: aggressive, hungry for power, and a games player. He or she may also be knowledgeable, and possess excellent managerial skills. But he or she will destroy much of the good work because the wrong set of characteristics is repeatedly recognized and rewarded. One of them is egotism, as you say."

"So the attitudes encouraged by the system also foster resistance to change?"

"More than resistance. Some go on the attack. I call these reactions antibodies. The ideas I introduce often represent a threat, so they're attacked, the way a foreign body is attacked in the bloodstream."

Zara let out a low whistle under her breath. "This is powerful stuff," she said. "But do you mean you would forego an account like that just because you don't like their attitudes? Can anyone be that much of a purist?"

"I'm not a purist, I'm a sleuth. I find the chinks in the armor of companies like this. The chinks are divisions that are very specialized, maybe, or not in the mainstream of company business. If I can start there, and make a success, that often proves to be my way in. Sometimes, I end up getting the whole company to play in harmony!"

"So you mean, you like to be conductor?" asked Zara. Her lip curled slightly, as she pounced upon a flaw in his virtue.

"Not all conductors are egotists," Stanley replied, reading her expression. "The best conductors know how to make the music speak for itself. They clear away imperfections so that soloists can stand out and the leaders can bring the best performance out of all the players. I can do that because I'm in a position to stand back, observe, and think. I'm paid to be objective, which most people working inside a company cannot be. Eventually, my aim is to remove enough flaws in the system so that people at all levels have more time to think and be creative."

"How?"

"By being less preoccupied with pressures, problems, and

crises. Ideally, each player is a soloist in his or her own way. Each one must excel. One violinist playing out of tune will ruin the whole piece." Stanley adjusted the paper-covered airline cushion behind his back, and looked at his watch. "If you don't mind, I'm going to sleep awhile."

As Stanley snoozed, with his window blind pulled down, Zara shone her personal spotlight onto her notes, and pondered her article. Stanley was a conundrum. People revered him. People reviled him. He could be sharp as a Swiss army knife one moment, and unable to answer a question the next. As for results—the bottom line—she really wasn't any clearer whether he achieved them or not. Maybe nobody could be sure. It was impossible to dismiss him as a fraud. Yet she couldn't guarantee that he was worth his fee either.

As the plane started to descend, Stanley woke up. He pulled open his blind to reveal early twilight outside. The plane was on time.

"Nice to know it's scarcely later than when we took off," said Stanley. There was a delighted expression on his face.

"Did you enjoy your nap?" asked Zara, observing him.

"It was very profitable," said Stanley, his grin expanding to Cheshire cat proportions. "I think I've come up with the answer to two problems that were preoccupying me."

"Oh?"

"It's lucky I went over those points about leadership with you. I realized that I was failing to look in the right place for the leader I need at Wellco. There is someone I can work with; very successfully, I believe, because he has a position with some autonomy, away from the main body of the organization. I missed him at first. It takes a little time to identify the people who will really get the job done."

The captain's voice came over the intercom, asking them to strap up for landing. "I think I've also got the answer to the question that young manager asked at the seminar," Stanley went on. "A leader . . . well, a leader moves."

"I don't think I understand." Zara was turning on her tape recorder, hoping that the high-pitched whistling of the engines would not cause too much interference.

"The kind of manager who can become a leader is always willing to move into uncharted waters, and to take other people along. Managers who are stuck in predesignated jobs are often doing what their predecessors did, and what their successors will do. True, they need to appear like movers and shakers, but they do this by skillful games playing.

"Leaders are more concerned with the health of the company than with their own status. Often they can be found lower down in the organization. They don't waste time politicking, so they're often overlooked. They are sustainers, as well as initiators. They have a vision, which they can communicate. But they can also maintain that vision, and consistently work toward achieving it. Often these people are not highly visible. They don't make a lot of noise. But they are to be found where things are steadily being achieved. As far as I'm concerned, they're the people I need to work with."

Zara looked skeptical. "Do these paragons of virtue really exist? And what is wrong with trying to gain position? Surely, competitiveness is a perfectly healthy human attribute."

"When it works on behalf of the company, yes. As everyone has been telling us, it's what we need most. But 'competitiveness' can be interpreted almost any way you want. You can't assume that a healthy motivation to do well oneself also means a sense of competitiveness for the company. In the workplace, between members of the same company, it can be more destructive than unfair trade tariffs or high interest rates. And it's endemic in American industry."

"But doesn't it usually add up to much the same thing: drive, willpower, an ability to get things done?" Zara murmured. She was scribbling as fast as she could, as the engine screamed louder.

"They're different. Promoting the company can mean doing things that are unpopular at first—such as making radical changes or taking risks. Things that will not necessarily bring the individual praise."

"So how can an individual get recognition? After all, don't we all need that?"

"Of course we do. But credit should be assigned where it's

due. I work on the basis that everyone's contribution can be valuable. Sometimes, extremely important suggestions have come from people working on the production line. They get recognition for those ideas. That's when they become willing to bust their asses to produce more. There's a powerhouse of human ingenuity inside every company."

The backward-thrust engines started to roar, and the plane lurched to a halt. Looking at her notebook, Zara realized that, even after three days, she still had not learned enough. Every time Stanley clarified one point, he introduced something else. There were still questions. . . .

* * *

Walking to the taxis, Zara wondered whether she would have to ask for more time, on the telephone at least, to clear up a few points. As she turned to ask him, Stanley wheeled away toward a newspaper stand. He picked up a financial newspaper, and leafed expertly to the page he wanted.

"Look," he said, grinning and holding up the graph and listings of the price-per-share index. "Here's an example of synchronous events for you—in more than one sense. This line on the graph represents Carwell, the company I told you about. It's a perfect example of a company that learned to fish. They did more with the right information than most could have done with land, capital, or control over people."

Zara peered at the chart uncomprehendingly. "I've worked with Carwell for seventeen months now," Stanley went on. "Their profits started to rise dramatically about five months ago. Now they're up there with some of the Fortune 500 companies. And this was an outfit that was hardly on the map when I first started there."

"How do you know you can take the credit?" asked Zara, still searching for worthwhile failings.

"I don't. The whole company gets it." Stanley grinned. "Except I do know that the bottom line started to look healthy shortly after the ideas I took in started to click there at all levels. Everyone started to play together, in the way I tried to describe to you over dinner. It was almost an organic process. There was resistance and some misunderstanding at first. But once things fell into place, everything started to change."

"Synchron—?" The question was drowned in an involuntary yawn.

"Could be," Stanley replied with a smile. "But we won't get into that now," he added quickly, seeing the expression of renewed journalistic inquiry on her face. "I'm glad to see you're so thorough in your research. But I'll give you references for anything else you need on the phone. Call me in a few days— let me know how the article's going." He smiled mischievously and turned on his heel. "But now I'm taking a short break, if you don't mind."

Before she could blurt out one more question, or her thanks, he was through the door and on his way home.

***

LESSONS FROM THE CONSULTANT'S STORY

Developing and Analyzing a System Is Essential

When he first meets Zara, Stanley emphasizes that old management principles about optimizing systems have contributed much, but have outlived their usefulness. A system can never be optimal because of randomness in the environment. Stanley says that as a consultant, he offers his clients paradigms based on the thinking of W. Edwards Deming. He tries to show companies that their systems, not their employees' incompetence, cause problems. Companies need to stop blaming the employees and to start examining their systems.

Companies can move in the right direction only when they take measurements and try to improve the system on an ongoing basis. Since the unexpected will happen, detailed planning for the future is futile. The former Airtread company made many mistakes: Managers would "force" results, and people saw lots of activity, so they thought the venture was successful. However, their margins were deteriorating, and they would not have survived long without the Zeeback takeover.

Stanley believes that we can take action by living in the present, by constantly examining our systems for flaws, and by looking for opportunities to remove complexity. Our methods for detecting flaws must be fine-tuned, because the causes of flaws can be subtle. For example, slight alterations in the proportions of ingredients in Zeeback's tennis racket frames caused major problems, and Stanley and the company's employees had to measure and make changes in the system for a year in order to make the products consistent.

Perhaps most subtle of all is the role that systems can play in fast-changing environments. What Gayle Palumbo and Wayne Goosens of Zeeback do not understand is that the company's most important repetitive activity is that of introducing new shoe products. They need to develop a real system for this critical task.

When conditions change rapidly, all employees, not just those in manufacturing, need a pattern to follow so that they get the right information when they need it. With Stanley to help people define their goals and roles, Zeeback will be able to cope with change. Stanley, unlike Gayle, knows that the entire work force must be informed and involved for this to happen.

For Discussion:

✓   How does Stanley help the designers cope with changing market conditions?

✓   How does this knowledge improve their situation?

Encouraging Change for Ongoing Improvement

What really makes people change? According to Stanley, it often takes a desperate situation to bring about a transformation of attitude and a willingness to do things differently. In the 1950's, when the Japanese listened to Deming, they had little to lose by trying his new ideas. Real change can be a slow and painful process, but in the face of a great threat, employees can overcome fractionalization, and everyone can begin to change.

Changing attitudes can ultimately result in higher productivity, but it is difficult for people to make that connection, which is why Gayle and Wayne believe that Stanley's methods are too "soft" and idealistic. In many cases, people at the highest company levels have the most trouble with change. Stanley notes in his Cleveland speech that these top managers have won the "game." They have the most power, recognition, and responsibility to lose.

Companies like Wellco represent a big challenge to Stanley. Most people at Wellco are so entrenched in their ways—egotism is rewarded there—that they cannot change without outside help. Even the quality-control people within the company are resistant to change. But even if they wanted change, they could probably not produce results fast enough for Wellco to remain competitive. This is where Stanley can be effective: by working to change attitudes, and providing the needed statistical tools.

For Discussion: Explain how Gayle's and Wayne's idea of making tactical changes differ from Stanley's approach of changing attitudes.

From Management to Leadership

Change requires faith and fortitude, according to the Japanese business leaders. One of the most important changes companies must make is allowing true leadership to flower. Leadership has nothing to do with management style. Many of today's managers are not leaders. Leaders inspire by their example and help the company develop a clarity and constancy of purpose. They can start a company down the road of reducing complexity, which leads to more cooperation and teamwork.

In his speech, Stanley comments that we have an incomplete understanding of how to identify and select leaders. One reason is that we confuse traditional attributes of management with leadership. Another reason, as Stanley explains to Zara, is that leaders are more concerned with the health of the company than with their own status within it, so they do not have high visibility. Even Stanley misses a potential leader at Wellco until he sorts out all his ideas.

Leaders are willing to risk moving into unknown territory, while managers "sit tight," stuck in the same routine, substituting "games" for action. Leaders have a vision. They can communicate what they learn, and they are able to encourage the company to be competitive with other companies, rather than having the people within the company compete with each other. Leaders understand that everyone must participate in striving for improvements, and that the credit for improvements goes to the entire company, not just to select individuals.

For Discussion:

✓   Can leaders be identified by their "style"?

✓   Why or why not?
✓   What can be done to help prevent potential leaders from being overlooked?

The Concept of Synchronous Events

The story begins with Stanley at his desk, pondering a phenomenon occurring at several client companies. He helps Carwell reduce complexity in a few areas, and besides improvements in these areas, improvements happen throughout the company. Stanley cannot explain the changes by simple cause and effect. Calling this somewhat mysterious phenomenon "synchronous events," Stanley theorizes that an unknown mechanism helps a company begin to behave like one organism.

Stanley's medicine (reducing complexity), administered to one or more limbs, acts on the entire body. Reducing complexity gives a company more leverage and allows for true teamwork and cooperation. Everyone's energy is then devoted to the company's purpose. The Japanese have long understood this idea. Carwell's results show what can happen when a company opens up and learns to make productive use of people and information.

For Discussion:

✓   How does the idea of synchronous events fit in with the concept of nonlinearity? with randomness and incomplete information? with other ideas of twentieth-century physics?
(Hint: There is no answer in the text. These ideas are still developing, and this question is meant to stimulate discussion.)

The Consultant's Role in Continuous Process Improvement

Each consultant in the continuous process improvement field offers something different from any other. The results a consultant achieves are important, but so is the information that he or she brings to a company. A good consultant acts as an objective resource for new information, bringing the latest thinking in from the outside world. Consultants are involved with a number of issues in companies, which is one reason it is difficult to judge the value of their work, as Zara learns.

Consultants are learning along with everyone else as new information becomes available, so it is unrealistic for companies to expect a consultant to have all the answers, or to perform a quick fix. The kind of consulting Gayle and Wayne want for Zeeback would shortchange the company and limit what could be accomplished. The business community often blames consultants for a company's problems. They are often accused of misguiding businesses: This is at least the premise, in the beginning, for Zara's investigative story.

Stanley works at a very deep level. He understands that quality and productivity are the results of making changes, not goals in themselves. Stanley offers companies information and a fresh perspective: that of an outsider who can objectively look at what is going on and guide people toward improvement. Stanley believes in continuous guidance so that improvements keep happening, and so that the people in the company "learn to fish." This way, the company gains even greater leverage as everyone applies the new ideas themselves.

Because Stanley's approach involves people at all levels and stresses group effort, he is bad news for egotists and those who want to keep credit for themselves. Taking credit is not consistent with the new ethos. While Stanley is proud of being the catalyst for change and improvement, he recognizes that everyone's participation is critical, and that credit for success belongs to everyone.

For Discussion:

✓   In what ways can a consultant exercise leadership? Is this role appropriate?

What Makes a Good Client?

Stanley spends considerable time and effort deciding whether to accept Wellco as a client. He tries to decide whether a company has basic qualities in place to benefit from his efforts. If a company is in a desperate situation, people will be receptive to listening to new ideas. In this case, external threats to the survival of the business may make a company a "good" client by default. Stanley would be in a position to do a lot of good in this situation.

In companies that are complacent, Stanley needs one or more leaders in place. These friendly allies could implement new ideas on a small scale, measure the results, and communicate the advantages to inspire others in the organization. In order for a client to be good, there must be people who can spread the consultant's ideas. The closer the allies are to top management, the better the client will be.

Faith, fortitude, and patience are key ingredients of a good client, who must be willing to change. People at the company must be open to using data to understand problems and make improvements. They must be willing to learn—not only specific tools and techniques, but how to learn. It is not easy to be a good client, but even the best consultants can only guide. The client must take ownership of the change process, its challenges, and its benefits.

AFTERWORD
Where Are We Now? What Next?

DEMING'S WORK ON SYSTEMS is based on modern theories of the world, particularly quantum physics, which describes the universe in terms of uncertainty, unpredictability, and randomness. The information needed to design an optimal system is unknown and unknowable. There will always be flaws. If we have been operating our businesses using Taylor's ideas, quantum physics upsets many commonsense notions.

How can we assess our present thinking to find out where we are on the journey from Taylor to Deming? As a start, we can compare their thoughts about crucial areas of business, in order to discover which philosophy we have been applying. It helps to express these ideas axiomatically as self-evident truths. As in geometry and other mathematical disciplines, axioms clarify the key points in complex bodies of knowledge. In the following sections, we list the key axioms for each philosophy, and point out their similarities and differences.

Axioms for Taylor's Philosophy

Taylor Axiom 1: Control of a business is established by staffing positions of responsibility and authority with professional managers trained in the theory of scientific management and systems analysis.

185

Taylor Axiom 2: Improvements are due to increasing the division of work, and increasing concurrency (different aspects of work being done at the same time), within a project or process, or among projects or processes.

Taylor Axiom 3: Develop systems to perform repetitive tasks.

Taylor Axiom 4: The optimum system can be created by the proper formulation of the objectives of the system and evaluation of alternatives to meet those objectives. The information will be available to create an optimum system.

Taylor Axiom 5: Once a system has been properly defined and installed, any failure to meet stated objectives must come from outside the system.

Taylor Axiom 6: Continuously monitor the status of the system for deviations from system objectives to see if improper worker selection, poor motivation, inadequate training, or weak supervision are the causes of missed objectives.

Axioms for Deming's Philosophy

Deming Axiom 1: Control of a business is established by leadership and cooperation.

Deming Axiom 2: Improvements are due to increasing the division of work, information, and creativity, and increasing concurrency (different aspects of work being done at the same time), within a project or process, or among projects or processes.

Deming Axiom 3: Develop systems to perform repetitive tasks.

Deming Axiom 4: No system is ever truly an optimum system: Every system must be analyzed to understand the natural behavior of the system and the variation of the system. Information for optimizing any system is unknown and unknowable.

Deming Axiom 5: Inconsistencies and contradictions, which become apparent upon analysis of the system, may be used to detect and isolate the built-in flaws of the system.

Deming Axiom 6: Create a secure environment so everyone can apply the first five axioms without fear. Offer support, reassurance, and appreciation.

Comparison and Contrast Between Taylor and Deming

Taylor believed in establishing the control of a business through people whose effectiveness derived from the power of their position. This approach is simply not viable today. In the modern organization, a leader's effectiveness depends less on credentials or position than on the trust and respect that he or she has developed within the organization. Nowhere has this been more compellingly demonstrated than in recent political events in Eastern Europe, where those in charge could no longer rule by entitlement or force.

According to Deming, management and leadership are not necessarily the same. Leaders can be any employees, at any level, who have a vision (or understand the organization's vision), and can lead others toward that vision. Decision-makers should understand the present situation, with respect to the organization's vision, before making decisions.

Axiom 2 simply recognizes the changes in paradigms for the way we accomplish work. Major paradigm shifts over the past three thousand years have included working together, creating products, developing materials separately from the products, interchangeable parts, designing systems (due to Taylor), and the maintenance and improvement of systems (due to Shewhart and Deming).

Each paradigm shift has significantly increased the division of work and the concurrency of that work while improving the effectiveness of the previous paradigms. The cumulative effect of these changes is responsible for the acceleration of technology development.

Axiom 3 recognizes that in both philosophies, the systematization of tasks can provide consistency of purpose, methods, and effort.

Taylor's assumption that an optimum system can be defined, and that there is enough information to define it, is directly contradictory to Deming's approach. Instead of trying to design an optimum system, Deming emphasizes the need to have a resilient system, which can be improved over time. Since external forces are always changing, the information needed to optimize any system is unknown and unknowable. The best one can do is to monitor the systems in place, and seek to use this information to make them better, given the natural chaos of the environment.

Since Taylor's approach assumes that the system is optimal, any failure to meet stated objectives must be due to forces outside the system. Since the major component outside Taylor's system is personnel, Taylor's approach tends to create situations of scapegoating and blame. In connection with the constant monitoring of people, this can create an environment of fear.

Since Deming's approach assumes that missed objectives are usually due to the system itself, it becomes possible to work on the system to make it better. This tends to encourage creativity and cooperation at all levels. Moreover, since the problems focus on the system, rather than the people, it is easier to avoid an atmosphere of fear and mistrust. It is this harnessing of the creativity and cooperation of the personnel, at all levels in any organization, that is the key to continual improvement.

The Next Step

Changing our worldview is very difficult, as the stories in this book have shown. It was not within the scope of this book to describe how the Deming approach can be implemented. Proper implementation requires learning to use statistical tools, and guidance on how and when to use these tools, from a statistician trained in the Deming approach. Unfortunately, there are very few mathematical statisticians who work on applied problems. Useful guidance from "theoretical statisticians," as Deming calls them, is hard to come by. A company needs to find a mathematical statistician who has come down from the ivory tower, and who understands what the real needs of industry are all about.

To help in this situation, a sequel to this book is planned, which will include further details of the axiomatic description of the Deming approach, material on leadership, an explanation of complexity, and how to reduce fear. While these are not the standard textbook topics for implementation, we have found them useful in our work.

Just as Deming gained understanding from physics, today's statisticians, and others, are looking for further insights arising from quantum theory. They are examining causality, continuity, and reductionism: assumptions questioned by the quantum theory. Who knows how many ways we can build upon Deming's ideas in the future? What we do know is that every company can improve its productivity now, by understanding and implementing Deming's philosophy as it exists today.

GLOSSARY

---

assignable causes   Another name for *special causes.*

bottleneck   The person, equipment, or procedure in an organization with the least capability of coping with the flow of materials, information, or work in the organization.

built-in flaws   Flaws that are present inside the *system,* frequently due to missing information at the time the *system* was developed.

burn-in   Testing a product under extreme conditions (usually heat) before shipment to a customer.

chaos   *Randomness* with a potential structure to it.

common causes   Factors inside the *system,* or inherent to the operation, which are responsible for most *variation* and are the result of *built-in flaws.*

complexity   There is no precise definition of complexity, but it can be described as system size in terms of: number of units, volume, dimension (smallness-largeness), time (short-long), deterministic or random *variation,* or context level (amount of information).

control chart   A graphic record of data that quantitatively describes a *system's* normal behavior and the *variation* in it. Control charts show typical behavior and variation over time.

cooperation   The attempt to understand a situation from several perspectives and the need for change before making decisions.

cosmology   A view of the universe. Assumptions on how the universe operates.

cycle time   The time taken to either develop or manufacture a product. Time required between the starts of successive cycles.

Deming   W. Edwards Deming, the American physicist and self-trained statistician who was instrumental in the economic recovery of the Japanese after World War II.

finished goods   Completed products waiting to be sold.

flow *vs.* capacity   Reducing the *variation* in product movement from one work station to another versus reducing the variation in throughput from one work station to another.

fractionalization   Occurs when people define a situation in such a way that someone else has the responsibility for it.

funnel demonstration   Dropping a marble through a funnel to try to hit a target, and then adjusting for error in different ways. This demonstration shows how *tampering* with a *system* increases the *variation* in a process.

hard quality *vs.* soft quality   "Hard" refers to the quality of the product itself, and "soft" refers to the processes that make and/or control the product.

Just-in-Time (JIT)   A logistical *system* of establishing a pre-determined inventory buffer for controlling the flow of materials or information between work centers within an organization. Originating in Japan, many Just-in-Time systems involve the use of *kanban* cards.

kanban   A way of implementing a *Just-in-Time* manufacturing *system*. The Japanese term meaning card control.

leadership   Giving people a picture of what needs to be done to achieve common objectives, and instilling the desire to achieve them. Most effective actions occur after clear visualization.

linearity   Manufacturing in a continuous mode and/or consistently adhering to a schedule.

MRP   The acronym for Materials Resource Planning. A computerized program that plans the flow of materials within a manufacturing operation. May reveal the inner workings of a company.

paradigm   An accepted philosophy or mode of thinking.

Pareto chart   A bar chart arranged in descending order of frequency.

pull system   A *system* used to supply or pull the production material on demand to meet customer requirements. *Just-in-Time* manufacturing is a pull production system that supplies product only on demand, which creates very little inventory.

push system   A manufacturing *system* in which product is moved or pushed to the next work station, whether or not that station can handle it. This creates large amounts of inventory.

quality   Improved consistency and reduced *variation* within the manufacture of a particular product.

randomness   The condition in which the order of an occurrence or the occurrence itself is by chance.

rollover   The time that it takes a manufacturing operation to change from producing one product to another.

Shewhart   Walter Shewhart, physicist and engineer at Bell Telephone, who acted as mentor to W. Edwards *Deming*.

special causes   Random, fleeting events outside the *system,* evidenced by atypical system behavior, which affect *variation* in the system.

SQC/SPC   Statistical quality control/statistical process control. SQC is the term used by the Japanese to describe the philosophy of W. Edwards *Deming*. SPC applies to Walter *Shewhart's* statistical techniques for controlling the consistency of the output of a process.

synchronous events   Related occurrences that happen at the same time, but have no measurable connection (often the connection does seem apparent).

system   A set of methods and procedures for performing repetitive tasks.

tampering   Changing a *system* without understanding its dynamics.

Taylor *or* Taylorism   The philosophy of Frederick Taylor, who developed a *system* called "scientific management" that covered the performance of repetitive tasks.

tooling   A pattern, procedure, or schedule to accomplish a specific task. For example, a photographic or mechanical template.

variation   Lack of uniformity in a *system* or the final product or service. Random changes within a manufacturing process so that different assemblies of the same product differ in quality. Variation indicates *complexity* and *built-in flaws.*

vendors *vs.* suppliers   A vendor is someone who sells, as does a hawker or peddler. This term is often used in a pejorative sense. A supplier is someone who furnishes what is needed. This term is often used in a positive sense.

Work-in-Process (WIP)   In a manufacturing operation, a product that has been started but is not in a form that can be sold.

working around   Trying to produce around missing resources such as material, procedures, information, and equipment. This tends to increase inventory.

ABOUT THE AUTHORS

DR. PERRY GLUCKMAN was president and founder of Process Plus, Inc., a network of statisticians and management advisors that guides companies in implementing quality improvement programs.

Dr. Gluckman received his Ph.D. in statistics from Stanford University. He held post-doctoral fellowships at the National Assessment of Educational Progress in Princeton, New Jersey and Denver, Colorado, and at the Center for Advanced Study in the Behavioral Sciences in Palo Alto, California.

In 1974, Dr. Gluckman began implementing Dr. W. Edwards Deming's philosophy at Lawrence Livermore Laboratories. In 1979, at the urging of Dr. Deming, he founded his own consulting business. A Deming authority, and published author of numerous quality and productivity articles, Dr. Gluckman died of cancer on January 28, 1992.

DIANA REYNOLDS ROOME is a journalist whose articles on a wide range of social issues have appeared in the United States, Britain, Canada, France, and Germany. Raised in England and educated at York and Oxford universities, she taught English literature and language to students in England and Nepal, and later worked as an editor of educational publications in London. She lives with her husband and two sons in Mountain View, California.